*T*his journal belongs to

_____

My
Strength and
My Song

ONE-YEAR
DEVOTIONAL
JOURNAL

BroadStreet
PUBLISHING

BroadStreet Publishing Group LLC
Racine, Wisconsin, USA
Broadstreetpublishing.com

My Strength and My Song
© 2016 by BroadStreet Publishing

ISBN 978-1-4245-5279-5 (flexi-faux leather)
ISBN 978-1-4245-5107-1 (e-book)

Devotional entries composed by Janelle Breckell, Diane Dahlen, Claire Flores, Laura Krause, Stephanie Sample, and Carole Smith.

All hymn lyrics quoted are listed in the public domain.

Design by Chris Garborg | garborgdesign.com
Edited and compiled by Michelle Winger | literallyprecise.com

Printed in China.

16 17 18 19 20 21 22   7 6 5 4 3 2 1

There's within my heart a melody
Jesus whispers sweet and low,
Fear not, I am with thee,
peace, be still,
In all of life's ebb and flow.

Jesus, Jesus, Jesus,
Sweetest name I know,
Fills my ev'ry longing,
Keeps me singing as I go.

Feasting on the riches of His grace,
Resting 'neath His shelt'ring wing,
Always looking on His smiling face,
That is why I shout and sing.

He Keeps Me Singing
By L. B. Bridges

Introduction

Take time each day to be refreshed and
strengthened by God as you engage your spirit in
these encouraging devotional entries, Scripture
· verses, and prayers.

Find hope, comfort, peace, security, and joy in the
Father who delights in singing over you as you rest
in his presence.

Be inspired as you record what's on your heart in
the journaling space provided.

The Lord is your strength and your song. He is
everything you need for each new day.

January

A joyful song of praise we sing,
And thankfully we gather
To bless the love of God above,
Our everlasting Father.

In Him rejoice with heart and voice
Whose glory fadeth never.
Whose providence is our defense,
Who lives and loves forever.

For nothing falls unknown to Him,
Or care or joy or sorrow;
And He whose mercy ruled the past
Will be our stay tomorrow.

A Joyful Song
BY A.N. BLATCHFORD

All Things New

He who sat on the throne said, "Behold, I make all things new."
And He said to me, "Write, for these words are true and faithful."
REVELATION 21:5 NKJV

The most beautiful thing about the God we've entrusted our lives to is that he makes all things new. That is a faithful statement—it has always been true and will always be true.

As we begin a new year, empty and full of both bright promise and worrisome unknown, we can rest our souls in the truth that our God will make everything new. Our regrets, mistakes, and failures are nothing compared to his covenanted promise of redemption and newness.

Thank you, Jesus, that you make all things new. Thank you that your Word is faithful and true, and I don't have to doubt your promises. Bring newness to my life this year. Take my regrets and turn them into new beginnings.

New Every Morning

The steadfast love of the Lord never ceases,
his mercies never come to an end;
they are new every morning;
great is your faithfulness.
LAMENTATIONS 3:22-23 NRSV

It is beautiful to know that the mercies of our God are new every single morning. To know that the grace we spent on yesterday will still be abundant enough for the troubles we will face today. To know that his faithfulness is true even when we wander, and his love is steadfast even when ours fails.

Heavenly Father, I know that I don't deserve the never-ending mercy that you extend to me. But I know that you delight in loving me and that you have more than enough strength for me in each and every new day. I pray that as I face today, I would walk as one who knows your faithfulness and understands your love.

Getting Back

As for you, return to your God,
hold fast to love and justice,
and wait continually for your God.
HOSEA 12:6 NRSV

Sometimes we lose our way and lose sight of the passion we once felt for God. Once we've lost our connection with him, we don't always know how to get back. We wonder if there is too much between us that he can't overlook.

But it's as simple as returning; as straightforward as getting down on your knees and saying, "God, I'm back." When you return, holding fast to the love that first drew you to him, God will show himself to you.

God, I know that there are areas of my life where I've put distance between myself and you. I don't want to continue with a disconnect between us. I want to return to you and be restored to right relationship with you. This is me, returning to you. Thank you that even when I wandered, you never went anywhere.

The Secrets of God

"Can you understand the secrets of God?
Can you search the limits of the Almighty?"
JOB 11:7 NCV

Have you ever discovered something about yourself that you never knew before? Maybe you tried a new food that you always claimed you hated, and you found you actually loved it. Maybe you were surprised by an idea you had that you didn't even know you were capable of.

If we, who are human, are so complex that we don't fully know ourselves, then how much more complex is the God who created us? We mustn't limit God to what we think we know of him. We cannot know his limits. But we can trust in his Word and his Holy Spirit to teach us as we seek to know him more.

Almighty God, help me not to limit you to what I've seen or what I've heard of you.
Help me to constantly be seeking your heart so that I can know you for myself.

The Yes To

The yes to all of God's promises is in Christ,
and through Christ we say yes
to the glory of God.

2 CORINTHIANS 1:20 NCV

We all go through seasons in life when we doubt if God is really good to us. But tasting the goodness of God is often as simple as opening our hearts to receive what he has promised through Christ.

We may feel unworthy or even unready, but if we have said yes to salvation, then we have also said yes to God's promises, his goodness, and his eternal glory.

God, I say yes, right now, to your promises for my life. I say yes to your glory, your goodness, and your grace. I thank you that your salvation and your promises are mine in Christ Jesus. I ask you for the strength to continue to say yes even when I feel ineligible. I know that in Christ I am a new creation who is worthy of goodness.

How to Fill Our Hunger

"I am the bread of life.
Whoever comes to me will never be hungry,
and whoever believes in me will never be thirsty."

JOHN 6:35 NRSV

You don't have to teach babies to put things in their mouth—they are born with a natural instinct to feed themselves. But you do need to teach them *what* to feed themselves.

We were all created with a natural spiritual hunger for God. But we must learn how to fill our hunger. There are things that we will try to put into our souls that will never satisfy us. The only true remedy to the deepest longing in our being is God—because we were created to hunger after him.

Lord, help me not to look to outside sources to fill the hunger that can only be satisfied by relationship with you. Help me to recognize my hunger so that instead of living as one who is empty, I can live as one who is full of your presence.

Powerful Words

*"Son of man, let all my words sink deep into your own heart first.
Listen to them carefully for yourself."*
EZEKIEL 3:10 NLT

There is so much power in quieting our minds and listening to the voice of God as he speaks directly to us. We must learn to recognize his voice above any other sound. God has the power and the ability to speak to any situation we are going through, under any circumstance.

Since the beginning of time, God has begun powerful works with a powerful Word. When we listen for him to speak, we ready ourselves for him to do those works in and through us.

Lord, I want to be someone who does powerful works for your kingdom.
I know that I cannot do them without the words from your mouth.
Let me be a listener who both absorbs your Word and is changed by it.

Standing at the Last

Lord, you are my God;
I will exalt you and praise your name,
for in perfect faithfulness
you have done wonderful things.
things planned long ago.
ISAIAH 25:1 NIV

We serve a God who at the end, after everything has fallen and everything has changed, will still stand. In all of our confusion, suffering, and hopelessness, we have the enduring promise of serving the one who will always be greater.

It's easy to become discouraged in this life, but when we adjust our perspective to view everything against the backdrop of a victorious Savior, we can face absolutely anything with great confidence and peace.

Thank you Lord that, in you, I can have the confidence of a victorious outcome—no matter how great the obstacles are that I am facing. Help me walk as one who is assured of my victory, trusting fully in my Savior who won it for me.

Water and Blood

This is He who came by water and blood—Jesus Christ;
not only by water, but by water and blood.
And it is the Spirit who bears witness,
because the Spirit is truth.
1 JOHN 5:6 NKJV

Jesus didn't come to earth only to save us—he also came to heal us. He takes us as we are, but doesn't leave us that way. Jesus came with water to cleanse us from our sin and to heal us from the inside out. He came with blood to sacrifice and to save us—trading his life for ours. Our salvation through Christ is complete as we are washed by the water and saved by the blood.

Thank you for your salvation, Lord. Thank you for not only saving me, but also healing me so that I can live an abundant life in your grace. Thank you for sending your Spirit who testifies of your great love to me—bringing your truth to my heart.

*O*ut of Darkness

But you are a chosen race, a royal priesthood, a holy nation,
a people for God's own possession, so that you may proclaim the excellencies
of Him who has called you out of darkness into His marvelous light.

1 PETER 2:9 NASB

Don't try to hide where you came from. No matter how dark or shameful your past was before you met Christ, there is power in your testimony. When a light is turned on in an already bright room, its effect is barely noticeable; but when even the smallest flicker of light appears in blackness, we are drawn to it.

We have been chosen as people of God's possession to proclaim his excellence and to be the visible evidence of his marvelous, life-changing light.

Thank you that you have called me out of darkness. Thank you that while darkness no longer defines me, I can testify about what I was saved from so that I can glorify who I was saved by.

Unpunished

He has not punished us as our sins should be punished;
he has not repaid us for the evil we have done.

PSALM 103:10 NCV

We deserve death, punishment, and distance from God because of our sin. But through the grace of salvation we have life, reward, and relationship with God. While the devil condemns us because of our sin and causes us to think that we have lost favor with God, the Holy Spirit convicts us of our sin and leads us to repentance and greater favor.

There isn't any condemnation for us in Christ Jesus because he died to remove our sin, our guilt, and our shame.

Thank you Jesus that, because of your death on the cross, I can stand blameless in the sight of Almighty God. I pray that I would be sensitive to the Holy Spirit's gentle conviction, but would overcome the devil's harsh condemnation because I am in Christ—a new creation, free of guilt and shame.

Do You Believe This?

"Everyone who lives and believes in me shall never die.
Do you believe this?"
JOHN 11:26 ESV

All throughout Scripture we are clearly promised eternal life through Christ. But there is something so poignant about the question in this verse: "Do you believe this?" Do you really, truly believe that you will live forever in heaven with Christ?

We are accustomed to promises being made and broken daily. Human fallacy has left us skeptical and anxious. But the beautiful truth is that we serve a God who will never back out of his covenant with us. Our hope of eternal life is sealed for us when we place our trust in Christ.

Thank you, Heavenly Father, for eternal life that is given to me through your Son. I do believe in you and in what you have promised me. Calm my fears and strengthen my faith. Enable me to live my life in you, relying on your strength and resting in your great love.

Accomplishment

Lord, you will grant us peace;
all we have accomplished is really from you.
ISAIAH 26:12 NLT

As we each look back on our lives, we remember what we've accomplished with some sense of pride. We have all climbed our mountains, but here we are—still standing to tell the tale.

As we reflect with peace in our hearts on things past, we must remember that we could have done none of it without God. He is the one who carries our burdens, comforts our hearts, strengthens our resolve, and orders our steps.

Thank you, Lord, that you have been there for me every step of the way. I would have nothing if it weren't for you. Thank you for the peace that you give me and for the works that you've done in me. I look forward to what you have yet to accomplish in my life.

Unseen

We do not look at what we can see right now, the troubles all around us,
but we look forward to the joys in heaven which we have not yet seen.
The troubles will soon be over, but the joys to come will last forever.

2 CORINTHIANS 4:18 TLB

It's not easy to fix our eyes on something we can't see. By abandoning our earthly perspective in exchange for a heavenly one, we are radically changed. If we are focused only on what is here on earth, we will quickly find ourselves overwhelmed by fear and uncertainty.

If we fix our eyes on the promise of heaven, then we cannot help but be filled with peace, joy, and hope. We must remember that while we are here on earth for only a little while, it is the joy of heaven that will be our eternal, blessed reality.

Lord, help me to fix my eyes on you and on eternity rather than on the momentary troubles around me. Give me your perspective.

aithful

Let us hold fast the confession of our hope without wavering,
for he who promised is faithful.
HEBREWS 10:23 ESV

We don't have to question whether or not God will do what he said he would. He has proven himself to be faithful and true. When God makes us a promise, we don't have to wonder if he will follow through. It is we who are forgetful, fearful, and oftentimes, faithless.

Through the power of the Holy Spirit, the truth of the Word of God, and the encouragement of fellow believers, we can hold fast to the hope of our salvation, staying true to the confession we made when we first believed.

Thank you, Lord, that no matter how much I wander, you remain faithful and true. Help me to hold fast to my salvation and to the hope I have in Christ Jesus. Thank you for your grace for my faithlessness and for your Holy Spirit who gives me the power to become faithful.

Measured Days

Lord, let me know my end,
and what is the measure of my days;
let me know how fleeting my life is.
PSALM 39:4 NRSV

Life throws all kinds of things at us. Stress, pressure, decisions, and busy schedules. When we are living, rushed in the midst of our own lives, we forget the age-old reality that life passes very quickly. If we stop—as the Psalmist did—in full awareness of a fleeting life, we begin to recognize that what was once pressing is really trivial, and what was once urgent is actually insignificant.

By numbering our days and being mindful of our own fleeting existence on earth, we can spend our energies not on the pressures of earth, but rather on the purposes of heaven, which will last forever.

Teach me, Lord, to number my days. Give me eternal vision so that I can live my life for the things that truly matter and not spend so much of my time pursuing what won't last.

Not Shaken

Cast your burden upon the Lord and He will sustain you;
He will never allow the righteous to be shaken.
PSALM 55:22 NASB

We all have different ways of dealing with worry. Some internalize it, others call a friend, and still others find a way to take their minds off it. When we bring our worry to God and lay our anxious hearts bare before him, he will encourage us, lift us up, and sustain us. He will not allow us to be shaken or weakened by worry because he holds us through every situation.

The God who knows beginning from end is not flustered by our anxiety, and does not allow us to be overcome by uncertainty.

Thank you, God, that you welcome me to come to you when I am burdened. You don't want me to carry my anxiety alone. My future is secure in your hands, and all I have to do is rest in you.

Never Disappointed

This hope will never disappoint us,
because God has poured out his love to fill our hearts.
He gave us his love through the Holy Spirit, whom God has given to us.
ROMANS 5:5 NCV

None of us are strangers to being disappointed. In life, we have learned to prepare ourselves for both the best and the worst possible outcomes. But when it comes to our salvation, there is no need to be braced for disappointment because the hope we have in Christ is guaranteed.

The presence of the Holy Spirit in our hearts reminds us constantly of this beautiful, certain promise we have in Christ.

Thank you, God, that the hope I have in you will not lead me to disappointment. No matter how many times I am let down in this world, I know that your love will never fail me.

Remember Your Wonders

I will remember the deeds of the Lord;
yes, I will remember your wonders of old.
PSALM 77:11 ESV

When we find ourselves doubting God's power to work miracles in our lives, we must remember the wonders he has performed throughout history. Scripture is full of accounts of lives changed by the power of God.

The same great God who raised Lazarus from the dead is the God we worship today. The God who gave sight to a blind man and who let a lame man get up and walk still works miracles. Believe God for something great, knowing that his power has never lessened and his wonders never cease.

God, I am amazed at the wonders you have performed throughout history. Help me to recall your power when I begin to doubt your strength. Thank you for redeeming me and allowing me, through faith, to witness your miracles in my own life. Help me to grow in faith and expectation of your greatness.

Because of the Poor

The Lord says,
"I will now rise up,
because the poor are being hurt.
Because of the moans of the helpless,
I will give them the help they want."
PSALM 12:5 NCV

God's economy is completely opposite from our own. Our currency is money and power, while his are mercy and grace. Our society elevates the rich and prominent, God lifts up the needy and nameless. His main objective isn't getting something from people; it's lavishing himself on them. His heart lies with the poor. He is a defender of the helpless and a protector of the weak.

If we desire to please the heart of the Father, then we too will take up the cause of the poor. We will defend them, rescue them, and help them. We will speak for them, honor them, and lavish love on them.

Father, I know that your heart is tender toward the needy.
Put opportunities in my path to meet the needs of the poor and to serve the helpless.

Fully Devoted

"Don't urge me to leave you or to turn back from you.
Where you go I will go, and where you stay I will stay.
Your people will be my people and your God my God."

RUTH 1:16 NIV

Ruth gave up everything she'd ever known to follow Naomi back to Bethlehem—a land completely foreign to her. What a radical commitment: to leave everything familiar for the sake of devotion to another!

Are you willing to leave everything you love and know to follow God? He is a God who rewards and repays. Everything you give up for the kingdom will be restored to you in an even greater measure than you gave up.

Heavenly Father, I want to be willing to go wherever you lead me—even if it takes me to places I've never been. You are my God, and I am fully devoted to you.

Human Empathy

Rejoice with those who rejoice, weep with those who weep.
ROMANS 12:15 ESV

There are few things more remarkable than the power of human empathy. When someone is hurt, we can feel their pain although we are not wounded. When someone cries, we can weep with them although we are not sad. When someone laughs, we can enjoy the moment with them although the happiness is not our own.

Jesus came to us, as a human, in the greatest act of empathy in history. As we follow his example by shouldering each other's sorrows and by sharing in another's joy, we express his heart to the world.

Lord, give me a capacity for empathy that will minister your character to those around me. Help me to better understand what others are going through so that I can reveal your heart to those around me.

To Have a Change, Make a Change

Do not conform to the pattern of this world, but be transformed by the renewing of your mind.
Then you will be able to test and approve what God's will is—his good, pleasing and perfect will.
ROMANS 12:2 NIV

We want change, but we struggle to get or stay on task with our goals. "One day, I'll…" is the enemy of "Today, I am…"; yet it seems that as long as change hurts more than staying the same, we vacillate between our desires and our comfort.

It is often so with surrendering to the Holy Spirit. He longs to do "greater things than these," and while this appeals to us, the comfort of doing nothing seems reassuring, safe, and predictable. We find, at last, that the center of God's will truly is the safest place for our lives. Knowing that, we revel in him as he molds and inspires us. We were created to do good things.

Thank you, Father, for the changes you are making in my life. I enjoy being transformed by you, polished like the silver brought out for special occasions. You are good to me.
Let your Word do the work in my life that you would like.

He Cares about You, Uniquely

Just as each of us has one body with many members, and these members do not all have the same function, so in Christ we, though many, form one body, and each member belongs to all the others.
ROMANS 12:4-5 NIV

Each of us has a function. We don't operate like one another because we aren't fashioned that way. We often don't agree upon priorities—beyond dwelling in Christ and living in love—because we are each made to carry different aspects of God's glory.

So often, we read this verse as an adjuration to play nicely with people of other denominations. That's not it, though. It's a glorification of our wondrously creative God, and an encouragement to each take up our gifts, allowing others to do the same. Our gifts are just as personal as our salvation experiences. When we finally embrace our interdependence, we honor each other and operate in unity. We embrace who we are in Christ and let go of what we are not. To have the liberty to do so is an aspect of what it is to be truly free in Christ, and to operate in freedom.

Father, thank you for the intricate care you used in making me. Help me to recognize what gifts within me are actually not universal values for everyone else, but are your unique signature of grace upon my life. I love you! Thank you for making me so thoughtfully, and letting me discover your hand on me. Your gifts are always good. Please show me how to foster what gifts you reveal throughout my day, today.

Leveling Up

Trust in the Lord with all your heart,
and do not lean on your own understanding.
In all your ways acknowledge him,
and he will make straight your paths.

PROVERBS 3:5-6 ESV

As we learn to walk in surrender to the Holy Spirit, our heavenly Father beckons us to a higher level of intimacy with him. In order to do this, we must become vulnerable and get real with him. We must continually trust him more than our experiences or reasoning.

When we trust God without boundaries, we find him more reliable than anyone else. We are wrapped in his love—the safest place we could find ourselves. Constantly leaning our hearts toward him, and choosing what he would, we receive his comfort and guidance, and our paths become straight.

Heavenly Father, I come to you and ask you to help me trust you, knowing that you have the best in store for me. Have your way with me. I release control, and I trust in you. You are for me, not against me. I love you.

Renewed Strength

I pray that the God who gives hope will fill you with much joy and peace while you trust in him.
Then your hope will overflow by the power of the Holy Spirit.
ROMANS 15:13 NCV

Life takes a lot out of us. From sickness and pain to uncertainty and sorrow, life's challenges can quickly drain us of our strength. But for those who have put their hope in the Lord, there is a source of refreshing.

For the one whose soul is tired and whose faith has all but dissolved, there is renewal to be found in Jesus. When we turn to the promises found in his Word and the joy found in his presence, we will be revived by his Spirit—finding strength greater than our own.

Thank you, Lord, that you offer a way for me to be strengthened in my weakness.
Help me to remember that true renewal can only come from your presence.

Freedom

It is for freedom that Christ has set us free.
Stand firm, then, and do not let yourselves be burdened again by a yoke of slavery.
GALATIANS 5:1 NIV

Christ paid a very high price for our freedom. With his life he purchased our salvation, and our emancipation from sin. When we choose to continue living in sin after our acceptance of Christ's work, it's as if a free man is willfully returning to bondage.

God's desire for us is that we live in complete freedom—freedom from sin, death, and the hopelessness of life without redemption. We must stand firm in the truth of our privilege, walking confidently in the freedom that was so dearly bought for us.

Thank you, Jesus, for the freedom I have in you. I pray that I would stand firm
and not give in to temptation or fall back into the bondage of sin.
I want to walk completely in the freedom that is mine in you.

Power to Transform

We are made right with God by placing our faith in Jesus Christ.
And this is true for everyone who believes, no matter who we are.
ROMANS 3:22 NLT

God has the power to transform anything. We may think that a person or situation is completely beyond redemption—but God can reclaim even the most impossible of hearts and circumstances. We may have lost faith in believing for something, but God never does because he knows what he is capable of.

God, who has the power to speak the universe into existence, can certainly intervene in a situation and have his way in it. God, who commanded the dead to walk out of a tomb, can surely soften the heart of even the most hardened soul.

Thank you, God, that you offer redemption for my heart, my life, and my circumstances. Help me to trust you fully in the redemptive process so that I can enjoy the benefit of a life that has been changed by you.

The Irony of Weakness

The Lord is the everlasting God,
the Creator of all the earth.
He never grows weak or weary.
No one can measure the depths of his understanding.
He gives power to the weak
and strength to the powerless.
ISAIAH 40:28-29 NLT

When you are stripped of your talents and strengths, you can do nothing but rely on the grace of God to carry you further. It is there, in your lacking, that God's power is truly revealed. None of us likes to feel inadequate, but if our inadequacy can further reveal Christ in us, it is always worth it.

We must remember that we are vessels of mercy—hallowed images of his grace that exist to always, first and foremost, bring glory to Christ.

In my weakness, Lord, be my strength. Reveal yourself through me so that I can join you in accomplishing your work.

Weight of Worry

Anxiety in a man's heart weighs him down,
but a good word makes him glad.
PROVERBS 12:25 ESV

Worry fills our head with questions that may never have answers and possibilities that may never come to pass. We become wearied as even our momentary troubles outweigh our peace. It is in these times that the encouraging words of a friend can become the catalyst to change our uncertainty into strength and our doubt into restored faith.

By surrounding ourselves with the type of people who regularly speak the truth, we unknowingly secure our own peace and future gladness.

God, when I begin to feel anxious, I pray that you would bring a friend to speak your truth to me. Help me also to be an encouraging friend who brings peace to those around me.

Joyful Remembrance

The Lord has done great things for us,
and we rejoiced.
PSALM 126:3 NRSV

We all have incredible stories to tell. These tapestries of our lives have been beautifully woven with a million moments of grace and wonder. Think back for a moment on some of the things God has done for you.

Your own remembrance of the miraculous amidst the ordinary will strengthen you as you rejoice in the great things he has done.

Thank you, Lord, for the great things you have done for me. Bring to mind all of the miracles—big and small—that have been worked in my life, so I can rejoice in your greatness and be strengthened by the word of my own testimony.

February

Again the Lord of light and life
Awakes the kindling ray,
Unseals the eyelids of the morn,
And pours increasing day.

This day be grateful homage paid,
And loud hosannas sung;
Let gladness dwell in ev'ry heart,
And praise on ev'ry tongue.

Ten thousand different lips shall join
To hail this welcome morn;
Which scatters blessings from its wings
To nations yet unborn.

Again the Lord of Light and Life
By Anna L. Barbauld

Guided

I will lead the blind by a road they do not know, by paths they have not known I will guide them.
I will turn the darkness before them into light, the rough places into level ground.
These are the things I will do, and I will not forsake them.

ISAIAH 42:16 NRSV

When you feel that you have lost your way, and your feet can't feel the path beneath you, God promises that he will lead you forward. Even if you can't see what lies ahead, and though the road feels rocky and unsure, God will guide you. The path that seemed impassable will become smooth and the way that seemed impossible will become straightforward.

God promises that he will do this for you and more—because he loves you and his is a love that never fails or forsakes.

Thank you for your promise to guide me no matter how impossible the way seems.

Set Apart Truth

"Sanctify them in the truth; Your word is truth."
JOHN 17:17 NASB

We are bombarded with falsehood daily. Tabloids tout lies about public figures, newspapers print inaccuracies, television shows muddy reality, and social media is crowded with articles that haven't been properly fact checked. But in a world of misinformation, there is one source of truth that we can always trust—the Bible.

When we don't know where to look to find truth, we can always open his Word and be strengthened by the certainty of it. We are sanctified—set apart—by the truth found in Scripture.

Lord, I need your truth. My mind is so full of the lies of the world that I find myself searching for the refreshing truth that can only be found in your Word. Set me apart by the power of your gospel. Free me from what is false and establish me in your truth.

God of Safety

Those who go to God Most High for safety
will be protected by the Almighty.
I will say to the Lord, "You are my place of safety and protection.
You are my God and I trust you."
PSALM 91:1-2 NCV

We all applaud the heroism of the young boy David when he took on the giant, Goliath. Or the boldness of Moses when he confronted Pharaoh about freeing the Israelites. But do we recognize that the same safety given to them has been given to us? They were regular people like us, who understood the power of the God they served.

Whatever you are facing right now, God is more than able to rescue you and keep you safe in the midst of it.

God, I want to have the kind of radical trust that these Biblical heroes had. Give me the boldness that I need to be a believer who walks in your power.

Him Alone

The Lord your God you shall follow, him alone you shall fear, his commandments you shall keep, his voice you shall obey, him you shall serve, and to him you shall hold fast.
DEUTERONOMY 13:4 NRSV

God is gracious and kind, but he is also a jealous God. He wants to be enthroned by hearts given completely to him. There are many conflicting demands on our devotion: causes that impassion us, ideas that excite us, and visions that energize us. While our efforts for these things are just, they can often distract us from the one purpose that should hold our allegiance.

It is God we should follow with more zeal than anything else. We must be willing to let go of everything in order to serve him more fully.

Lord, I want you to be my one true passion.
Let my devotion to you be the defining cause of my life.

Cleansed

Have mercy upon me, O God,
According to Your lovingkindness;
According to the multitude of Your tender mercies,
Blot out my transgressions.
Wash me thoroughly from my iniquity,
And cleanse me from my sin.

PSALM 51:1-2 NKJV

We should all long to be purified of our sin because it is in the cleansing from our iniquity that we are brought nearer to God. Our sin may be precious to us, but when we compare it to the treasure of closeness with the Father, it instantly loses its worth.

God doesn't harden his heart to a repentant believer. When we cry out to him in genuine remorse, he lavishes us with his mercy and love, washing us of our sin and restoring us to right relationship with him.

Have mercy on me, God. Remove my sin from me and cleanse me so that I can be closer to you.

Without Fear of the Future

She is clothed with strength and dignity,
and she laughs without fear of the future.
PROVERBS 31:25 NLT

It's natural to fear the unknown. It can be frightening not to know what's coming or how to prepare for it. But you don't have to fear the future when you know whom you trust. You can live without anxiety about what is to come because you know that your life is in the hands of the one who controls it all.

When you are in Christ, you can smile at the mystery of the future with the peaceful and carefree heart of one who knows it is secure.

God, give me the strength to smile at the days to come. Don't let me waste my moments in fear of things that fear can never change. Grant me the peace that comes with trusting you.

A Greater Wonder

When I look at your heavens, the work of your fingers,
the moon and the stars, which you have set in place,
what is man that you are mindful of him,
and the son of man that you care for him?

PSALM 8:3-4 ESV

The greatness of our God is displayed majestically throughout his creation. When we look into the night sky at all the twinkling stars and the far off planets, we realize almost instantly how small we are in his universe. But a greater wonder than the grandeur of God's capacity is his value for mankind.

The God of all this—the universe and everything in it—is the same God who gave his life to know us. The God who spoke the world into being is the same God who speaks quietly to our hearts. His love for us is as unsearchable as the heavens.

Father, I don't understand why you love me the way you do when you are as great as you are. But I am so thankful you do.

Fully Committed

"May your hearts be fully committed to the Lord our God,
to live by his decrees and obey his commands, as at this time."
1 KINGS 8:61 NIV

Is your heart fully committed to God? Or are other loves claiming your devotion? If your heart has truly been given to the Lord, then you will naturally follow his commands with your life. To be committed to someone is to be driven by a desire to please them—to give them your best because your own love demands it of you.

Regularly examine your heart to evaluate whether or not your full commitment lies with God, or if you are allowing your heart to become distracted by another love.

Lord, give me a heart that is fully committed to the love of you and a life that is fully devoted to following your way. I want to be true to you—even when sin threatens to divide my heart.

Trustworthy

For the word of the Lord holds true,
and we can trust everything he does.
PSALM 33:4 NLT

All of us have experienced our fair share of hurt. We've been jaded by failed dreams, broken relationships, and empty promises. No matter how hurt or worn down we may feel, we can always trust God with our hearts. He will never lie to us, manipulate us, or let us down. He will never go back on his word to us, abandon us, or stop loving us.

The Lord is always true to his Word. Who he has been throughout the ages is who he remains today. The God we read about in Scripture—who never forgot his covenants and loved irrevocably—is the same God who holds our hearts today.

Thank you, Lord, that in a world where trust is broken daily, I can always trust you perfectly. Please heal my heart from the hurt I've experienced so that I can love you more deeply.

FEBRUARY 10

Go in Peace

Then He said to the woman, "Your faith has saved you. Go in peace."
LUKE 7:50 NKJV

Each time after Jesus healed someone, he gave them the same command: "Go in peace." Jesus knew that even after the wonder of the miracle, there would be questions. Though outer healing had been given, inner turmoil would still threaten to overwhelm their hearts.

When Jesus heals someone, he heals them wholly. He doesn't just fix one problem, he saves the whole person. When we come to Christ, we are healed from the laws of sin and death and brought into a life of wholeness and peace. Our peace is a mark of our healing and we must walk confidently in it.

Thank you, Lord, for the peace that you've given me. I don't have to be shaken by the fear or turmoil of my sinful nature because you have healed me and sent me forth in peace.

48

Fascination

Those who love your teachings will find true peace,
and nothing will defeat them.
PSALM 119:165 NCV

The natural result of love is fascination: to be drawn to something so irresistibly that nothing can keep you from it. When we fascinate ourselves with the Word of God, we become an indestructible force in the spiritual realm.

We cannot be easily subjected to the lies of the enemy when our hearts have been saturated in the truth. By loving the teachings of God, his wisdom becomes our confidence and his presence our reward.

God, give me a love for your teachings. When my flesh rises up against your truth, help me to overcome it by your Spirit. Let me be fascinated by you. Give me a love for you and your Word that is unmatched by any other love in my life.

Joyfully I Wait

I wait for the Lord, my whole being waits,
and in his word I put my hope.

PSALM 130:5 NIV

We so often think of waiting as hard, even unpleasant. But sometimes, waiting is wonderful: waiting to deliver great news, waiting for the birth of a child, the anticipation of giving a special gift.

When the thing we wait for is a good thing, waiting itself is a gift. This is how it is to wait for the Lord. With all our hope in him, the outcome is certain. The outcome is eternity. Let every part of us wait on him in joyful anticipation.

Lord, I love waiting for you! Because I know you bring only goodness, I can wait for you forever.
Your Word is my hope, and it promises life and light forever with you.
Gratefully, joyfully, I wait and I hope.

Though We Stumble

The Lord makes firm the steps
of the one who delights in him;
though he may stumble, he will not fall,
for the Lord upholds him with his hand.

PSALM 37:23-24 NIV

Recall a near miss or two. The accident that almost happened, the plane you almost missed, the storm that began just a few seconds after you made it inside. Adrenaline pumping, we may forget to thank God for that extra boost of speed or the extra stopping power of our brakes.

Did we really "almost" fall, or were we given a glimpse of the Lord at work in our lives? As humans, we stumble; as his children, we are caught.

Lord, I see. I see that an *almost disaster* is actually a window into your love for me. You never let go of my hand. I stumble because I am human. I remain upright because I am yours.

Good and Perfect

Whatever is good and perfect is a gift coming down to us from God our Father,
who created all the lights in the heavens. He never changes or casts a shifting shadow.

JAMES 1:17 NLT

Take the next few minutes to pause and consider all the good, all the beauty in your life. You may be in a season that makes this easy, or perhaps now is a time that doesn't feel particularly "good and perfect."

Peonies in June, the wink of a quarter moon, loving and being loved, these are gifts from God. Your Father is a good father, a giver of good gifts. This doesn't change, even when your circumstances do.

Lord, every day you send gifts, reminding me you are good and I am yours. Help me see your gifts even through tears. You are constant; you are perfect. Thank you for loving me.

Tears Turn to Joy

Those who sow in tears
shall reap with shouts of joy!
PSALM 126:5 ESV

In times of sadness, whether from a fresh heartbreak or the memory of a distant one, it can seem like the pain will never end. No words of comfort, no matter how true or well-intentioned, can take away the ache.

These are the times we need only to crawl into our Abba's lap and allow his love and promises to envelop us in comfort. He won't say when, but he does assure us: we will shout again for joy.

Father, there are days it is just too much. This world brings so much diculty, challenge, and sadness, I just want to lie in your arms. How wonderful to know that I can! You hold me tightly and whisper your promises in my ear: "You will laugh again, daughter. You cry today, but one day, you will shout for joy."

Not of the World

> "My prayer is not that you take them out of the world but that you protect them from the evil one. They are not of the world, even as I am not of it."
>
> JOHN 17:15-16 NIV

When something is too wonderful to describe, we say it is "out of this world." It is clearly from here, but something sets it apart as special.

It's the same way with us. We still go to our jobs, sleep in our beds, and do our best to love well and make a difference, but there is something different about those who belong to Jesus. We are no longer of this world. That makes us both special and vulnerable.

Lord, though I long to be called out of this world and home to be with you, I know I belong here for now. Stop the enemy at every turn as he tries to keep me from shining your light.

Under His Protection

If you make the Lord your refuge, if you make the Most High your shelter,
no evil will conquer you; no plague will come near your home.
For he will order his angels to protect you wherever you go.

PSALM 91:9-11 NLT

Safety is big business. Consider all the product lines that exist to protect us: everything from sports equipment to security systems. For nearly every aspect of life, someone has a way to make you safer in it.

God knows our desire for security, and he offers protection like no amount of padding or technology could ever provide. He's got our eternal souls under his wing.

Father, you are my safety from life's storms or even my own mistakes. I find shelter in your protection. What joy I feel when I realize I have nothing to fear! Because I love you and choose to stay close to you, I can sing for joy all my days.

People of Light

Once you were full of darkness, but now you have light from the Lord. So live as people of light! For this light within you produces only what is good and right and true.
EPHESIANS 5:8-9 NLT

On an x-ray, a dark spot represents something that shouldn't be there. A tumor, a clot, a crack in the bone. For our bodies to function as they're meant to, these dark spots require attention and removal —before they can harm us further.

Sin is a dark spot on our hearts. Jesus is the life-giving light that obliterates those dark places and makes us healthy and whole. He allows us to be people of light, reflecting his goodness and proclaiming his truth.

Lord, I was filled with darkness but you obliterated it with your light. Even when sin tempts me, your light works in me and through me, leading me back to goodness and truth.

FEBRUARY 19

Truly Awesome

The heavens declare the glory of God;
the skies proclaim the work of his hands.
Day after day they pour forth speech;
night after night they reveal knowledge.
PSALM 19:1-2 NIV

Amazing beauty is all around us, so much so that we can become used to it. When was the last time you stopped to marvel at God's incredible creativity? Study a flower. Read about the human eye. Watch the sun rise or set. Write down your dreams. Spend some time just soaking in the awesomeness of the creator.

God, you are truly awesome. Every time I look at the sky, I see something new. Even a few attentive minutes on this earth reveal miracle and majesty everywhere I look. How beautiful you have made this world, and how blessed I am to live in it.

57

All of You

> "Love the Lord your God with all your heart and with all your soul
> and with all your mind and with all your strength."
>
> MARK 12:30 NIV

Do you know how desperately the Father loves you? Replacing the myriad rules of the Old Testament, Jesus asks us to keep one beautiful commandment: love God with your entire being. He wants to be loved with your heart, your soul, your mind, and your strength. Which of these do you find yourself most reluctant to give to him?

Lord, I give you my heart. Let all my passions and desires come from you. Father, my soul is yours. In the deepest, most eternal part of me, I commit myself to you. Jesus, take over my mind. Replace my temporal thoughts with the things that matter to you. Spirit, use my strength for your purposes. I love you, and give you all that I am.

_____

_____

_____

_____

_____

_____

_____

_____

_____

Rocks Don't Change

Trust in the Lord forever,
for the Lord, the Lord himself, is the Rock eternal.
ISAIAH 26:4 NIV

When people talk about the most dependable person they know, they may describe that person as being their rock. These people represent a constant in our lives; the advice they give today is the same advice they'll give in twenty years. Their principles—and their love—are unwavering.

A rock placed in a box for decades will look exactly the same on the day it's rediscovered. Rocks don't change.

Lord, you are the rock eternal. I trust you with my life, Father, because I know your commitment to me is unwavering. I am safe with you. You want what you have always wanted; you are who you have always been. You are constant. You are good. You are love itself.

Rest for Your Soul

"Take my yoke upon you and learn from me, for I am gentle and humble in heart,
and you will find rest for your souls. For my yoke is easy and my burden is light."
MATTHEW 11:29-30 NIV

Choose a job: breaking up and moving rocks to prepare a field, or scattering seeds behind the plow. Back-breaking labor or a semi-leisurely stroll?

Jesus' invitation to walk with him is just such a choice. His way is love, trust, and dependence on the Father. Our way is, well, more like breaking up rocks. When he invites us to follow him, he invites us to lighten our loads.

Lord, help me to accept your yoke. You oer protection and grace; your way is peaceful. My way represents struggle as I wrestle against things far too heavy for me to bear alone. Humble my heart, Jesus so I can rest my weary soul.

Nothing to Fear

In the multitude of my anxieties within me,
Your comforts delight my soul.
PSALM 94:19 NKJV

Worry. Stress. Anxiety. Chances are, just reading those words heightened your own levels of each. Fear is one of the greatest threats to the peace we have in the Lord.

As we become consumed by the many pressures of this world, it's easy to take our eyes off the comforter of our soul: God's Holy Spirit. Just as easily, let us turn back to him and watch our many worries fade into insignificance.

Lord, I confess I have a multitude of anxieties. I know that as your child there is nothing to fear, but pressures from this world turn me from the truth and cause me to focus on my worries. Thank you for your endless comfort, Father. In your arms I find peace. You delight my soul.

Completely Attuned

When I said, "My foot is slipping,"
your unfailing love, Lord, supported me.
PSALM 94:18 NIV

A good surgical assistant knows what instrument the surgeon needs before they ask for it. A mother can spot a stuffy nose or broken heart the minute her child enters the room; the right words and a hug are waiting. Attentiveness: it's part of the job.

The Lord is completely attuned to your needs. Long before you fall, his arm waits to steady you. He's right here with you, always.

Lord, your attentiveness humbles me. I slip, and I find your arm waiting. I stumble, and you steady the ground beneath me. You are unfailing, despite my many failures. Thank you, Father, for knowing me and loving me so perfectly.

Peace with God

Since we have been justified through faith,
we have peace with God through our Lord Jesus Christ.
ROMANS 5:1 NIV

Do you ever wonder if you please God? Sometimes this question rolls around in a believer's mind, subconsciously or consciously. For a child of God, it's a rather easy answer. We need to train our hearts and minds with the answer so we don't needlessly torment ourselves.

There is one way alone to peace with God. If you have received Christ as your Lord, then the faith it took you to believe that justified you before God. Your faith in Christ makes you no longer guilty. Because of that, you can have peace. Dear child, don't wonder. God is not like us—fickle and hard to please. He is pleased with his Son's sacrifice and your faith in it.

Help me, Jesus, to remain in your peace.

He Will Fulfill His Purpose for You

The Lord will fulfill his purpose for me;
your steadfast love, O Lord, endures forever.
Do not forsake the works of your hands.
PSALM 138:8 ESV

Did you know God is more intent on fulfilling his purpose for your life than you are? He is fully aware you are the weaker vessel in your relationship with him. While we might have zeal and passion, we naturally grow weak, lazy, or idle. This can be discouraging to us, but God is not easily discouraged. After all, he is our Maker and knows exactly how frail we are.

God can fulfill his purpose for you because his love will endure over you forever. It is not a weak love. You are the precious work of his hands.

God, help me trust you and partner with you in fulfilling your purpose for my life. Thank you that you made me with a purpose and I am not a mistake.

Life Is a Pilgrimage with God

Blessed are those whose strength is in you, whose hearts are set on pilgrimage.
As they pass through the Valley of Baka, they make it a place of springs;
the autumn rains also cover it with pools. They go from strength to strength,
till each appears before God in Zion.

PSALM 84: 5-7 NIV

The Psalmist gives us a picture of what it is like to be on a pilgrimage with God. Every Christian begins their journey as a pilgrim, and it doesn't end until we are with him forever. Anyone who has walked even a little way on this journey knows the pilgrimage is not always—or ever—a smoothly paved path. There are mountaintops and valleys.

Another name for *Valley of Baca* is *Valley of Weeping*. Just because we are headed to Zion does not mean we won't struggle. For the believers who continue, they will see that they aren't getting weaker but stronger. This is because the longer they walk, the more they learn their strength isn't in themselves.

Thank you, Lord, for starting me on this pilgrimage.
As I grow weaker physically, thank you that you are making me stronger spiritually.

Rooted in Love

You, O Lord, are a God merciful and gracious,
slow to anger and abounding in steadfast love and faithfulness.

PSALM 86:15 NRSV

It is so important, as God's children, that we are confident in his character. In Ephesians 3:17, Paul prays that we be rooted and established in God's love. This means our roots are buried deep in the soil of his love, and we drink all our sustenance through those roots.

As you remain confident of his love, you can receive correction and direction from him without offense because you know it comes from a heart of love.

Thank you, God, that you are slow to get angry. You aren't quickly annoyed or angered. Your love toward me is steady and constant. Help me to stay rooted in your love.

March

Always with us always with us
Words of cheer and words of love,
Thus the risen Savior whispers,
From His dwelling place above.

With us when we toil in sadness,
Sowing much and reaping none,
Telling us that in the future
Golden harvests shall be won.

With us when the storm is sweeping
O'er our pathway dark and drear,
Waking hope within our bosoms,
Stilling ev'ry anxious fear.

With us in the lonely valley,
When we cross the chilling stream—
Lighting up the steps to glory,
With salvation's radiant beam.

Always With Us
By E. S. Carter

Unconditional Acceptance

Accept one another, then,
just as Christ accepted you,
in order to bring praise to God.
ROMANS 15:7 NIV

If she gossiped less. If he shared his feelings more. It's easy, isn't it, to list the ways other people could change for the better? We know we are called to live in harmony with one another, but our "others" can really make it difficult.

But we need to accept one another...as Christ accepted us. Jesus takes us as we are: broken, imperfect, sinful. If this is how the Savior welcomes us, who are we to put conditions on our acceptance of anyone else?

Lord, thank you for accepting me just as I am. You see past my many flaws and you love me for me. Help me to see others as you see them and to glorify you through unconditional acceptance.

Ready to See

Open my eyes that I may see
wonderful things in your law.
PSALM 119:18 NIV

Think back to a time you suddenly understood something. Maybe you were late to get the punchline of a joke, or maybe you finally understood why your mom wouldn't let you wear something to school. "Oh…I get it!" you said.

The Bible is filled with "Aha" moments. As we go deeper into the Word, God opens our eyes to things we never noticed before. Stories we've heard all our lives become fresh with new insights. Truths we've taken for granted take on new weight and significance as we discover the Word is alive.

Father, open my eyes. Show me the beauty and depth you've hidden within your Word.
Surprise me with wisdom; delight me with understanding. I'm ready to see.

A Heart That Cares

God is working in you, giving you the desire and the power to do what pleases him.
PHILIPPIANS 2:13 NLT

What was your last random act of kindness? Whether you bought a homeless man a burger, donated to dig a new well in Africa, or simply smiled at a stranger in the produce aisle, these impulses are evidence of the Spirit at work in your life.

The more we tune into God, the more he will work in us. As we focus our thoughts on his perfect love and look to him for inspiration, he provides us with opportunities—big and small—to express his love to others.

God, today I thank you for giving me a heart that cares. Help me to see and to seize the opportunities you place before me to share your love and goodness, today and every day.

Twig by Twig

The wise woman builds her house,
But the foolish pulls it down with her hands.
PROVERBS 14:1 NKJV

If you were to see a mother bird ripping her nest apart, how would you react? It's hard to imagine, isn't it? Now consider a woman you know who is too busy to attend a soccer game, return a phone call, or write a sympathy card. Sadly, it's not so hard to imagine. Maybe you even saw yourself.

Choice by choice, twig by twig, we have the option to build our homes, our lives, our relationships, or destroy them. When we keep our attention on the Father, he gives us the strength to keep building.

Father, remind me today of what matters most. Help me to be a builder, reinforcing my connectedness with the people I love. Grant me wisdom and strength in Jesus' name.

Just Because

Honor the Lord for the glory of his name.
Worship the Lord in the splendor of his holiness.
PSALM 29:2 NLT

It isn't your birthday, but there's a gift on the counter with your name on it. You haven't done anything particularly special lately, but a card arrives in the mail to let you know you are loved—just because. It feels wonderful. It feels even better when you are on the giving end.

When is the last time you worshipped God just for being God? He loves to receive spontaneous gifts of love, honor, and praise just as much as we do.

Lord, above all other names, I worship yours. I meditate on your holiness, your perfection, and it brings me to my knees. I love you, God, for who you are and I thank you for who you are helping me to become.

Sight Unseen

Though you have not seen him, you love him; and even though you do not see him now, you believe in him and are filled with an inexpressible and glorious joy.

1 PETER 1:8 NIV

How did you first fall in love with Jesus? Unlike human love, one of the great mysteries of faith is how we can know so surely and love so deeply he whom we've never actually seen. But we can. We do.

One of the great rewards of faith is the "inexpressible and glorious joy" the Holy Spirit places in our hearts the moment we believe. Have you claimed your joy today?

Father, as I meditate today on all the ways I know you are real, allow your Spirit to fill me once again with the inexpressible, glorious joy that comes only from loving you.

_____

_____

_____

_____

_____

_____

_____

_____

_____

Cookie Jar Prayers

If my people, who are called by my name,
will humble themselves and pray
and seek my face and turn from their wicked ways,
then I will hear from heaven,
and I will forgive their sin and will heal their land.
2 CHRONICLES 7:14 NIV

Even young children understand cause and effect. "If I am naughty, I get a time out. If I say please, I get a cookie." Often, we approach prayer with the same way.

"If I pray, he listens." But does he? We must humbly seek his face and turn from our sins so we can be forgiven and heard.

Lord, I confess today my "cookie jar" prayers, thinking that if I say please, you'll say yes. Humbly, Father, I seek your face today. I turn my back on my sins and ask to be heard.

He Never Sleeps

He will not let you stumble;
the one who watches over you will not slumber.
PSALM 121:3 NLT

How long can you go without sleep? Most of us have gone all night at least once, but we also collapsed, exhausted, as soon as we were able. No matter how important the task, how critical the vigil, we all have to take a break eventually.

All except God. The one who watches over you, the one who makes sure you won't stumble as you climb today's mountain, never stops watching. Always and forever, night and day, he's got you.

Father, I marvel today at the realization that you never take your eyes o me. You have my eternity in your heart, and you won't let me fall. Whatever my mistakes, you are awake and ready to guide me back to the right path. Thank you, Lord, for your constant presence.

No Darkness

This is the message we have heard from him and declare to you:
God is light; in him there is no darkness at all.
1 JOHN 1:5 NIV

In total darkness, we instinctively seek light. We turn on our phones, fumble for a light switch, light a candle. With a single light source, the darkness can be overcome. We can find our way.

This same principle applies to our hearts. God is pure light, and with him, we can overcome any darkness we face. No temptation, no addiction, no sin is too powerful for God to conquer.

Father, I know that whenever and wherever I face darkness, I need only seek your face. You are all good, all pure, all light. I surrender my struggle with the darkness to you, and ask you to help me overcome it. I want to live in your pure light.

He Chose You

The Lord is all I need. He takes care of me.
My share in life has been pleasant; my part has been beautiful.
PSALM 16:5-6 NCV

If you are a follower of Christ, God chose precisely when and how to invite you to join his family. You received the most prestigious, coveted invitation in history. He chose you.

Maybe you simply yearned for more meaning in your life and he led you into a Christian community. Perhaps you needed a radical life change, to shed an addiction or other destructive pattern, and you felt him lift you out of the darkness. Regardless of how it happened, he called you by name, and now you are his.

Lord, I'll never get over it: you chose me. You pulled me out of darkness, into light and love and hope. I am yours, today and forever. Thank you!

Hidden Treasure

He opened their minds so they could understand the Scriptures.
LUKE 24:45 NIV

It's amazing, isn't it, to watch a movie or read a book you remember from childhood and see all you missed back then? Like uncovering hidden treasure, our adult minds understand bits of humor, layers of context and subtext in a way we couldn't as children.

When it comes to our faith and our understanding of the Scriptures, we are all as children. God chooses what to show us and when, so like that favorite childhood story or film, the Bible can feel brand new every time we return to it.

Lord God, again I ask you to open my mind. Every day, show me more in your Word so I can know you and please you. Thank you for your Word and the treasures you've hidden within.

More of You

"He must become greater; I must become less."
JOHN 3:30 NIV

Imagine you're famous. People follow you, listen to you, and genuinely respect you. Now, imagine willingly, even happily giving it all up. How did that feel? For most of us, sacrificing that fame wasn't easy—and it wasn't even real. Humility is hard. It's also a requirement for a Christ-centered life.

John the Baptist, one of the most truly humble people in all of Scripture, spoke the words of John 3:30. He knew it was time for Jesus to fulfill the prophecies, which meant it was time for him to point others toward Jesus—and away from himself.

Lord, help me to set aside my own agenda, my own desires, and to allow you to increase your influence in my life. When people look at me, may they see increasingly more of you.

An Incomprehensible Gift

When people work, their wages are not a gift, but something they have earned.
But people are counted as righteous, not because of their work,
but because of their faith in God who forgives sinners.

ROMANS 4:4-5 NLT

No matter how much a person loved their job, if their employer stopped paying them, they'd eventually stop working. Conversely, if the employee stopped working, the employer would inevitably stop signing paychecks. In an employment agreement, both parties have to honor their part for it to work.

This is what makes our relationship—our mutual agreement—with Jesus so astonishing. His part of the agreement was death on a cross to ensure our salvation. Our part is belief.

Lord Jesus, I will never deserve your sacrifice. No matter how hard I work,
I will never even the scale. Today, I thank you for the incomprehensible gift of my salvation.

Where Are You?

Then the Lord God called to the man, "Where are you?"
GENESIS 3:9 NLT

When adults play hide-and-seek with children, they usually know exactly where the kids are hiding. Still, they play along for the benefit of the little ones. "Where could she be?" they playfully wonder aloud. The period of life when we believe we can hide in plain sight is brief, and full of discovery.

When Adam and Eve first sinned, God took on a similar role. He knew exactly where they were (and what they'd done), yet he called to them, "Where are you?" In order for them to begin the healing process, they first had to realize—and confess—where they were.

Father, I make the same mistakes over and over, yet you allow me to discover them for myself. Patiently, you wait for me to come out of hiding, to return to your arms. Thank you.

He Holds My Hand

I, the Lord your God, hold your right hand;
it is I who say to you, "Fear not,
I am the one who helps you."
ISAIAH 41:13 ESV

Looking back on the hardest, scariest things we've ever done, we often wonder where we found the courage. How on earth did we face that diagnosis, pass that exam, give that eulogy?

Scripture assures us our help comes from heaven, from God himself. He is the inner voice saying, "You can get through this. You are strong enough." That sudden burst of strength, bravery, or initiative? That was the Lord, squeezing your hand.

Lord, how amazing it is to me to realize you hold my hand. You never let me go.
The courage, the strength, the power that seems to come from nowhere—it all comes from you.
You are my constant help, and the only help I need.

Not for Nothing

I do not set aside the grace of God,
for if righteousness could be gained through the law,
Christ died for nothing!
GALATIANS 2:21 NIV

For weeks, you've prepared. Extra study sessions, flash cards, copious notes. Finally, you're ready. You enter the classroom and see this message: "Test canceled. Everyone gets an A." All that work. All for nothing.

If we believe we can get to heaven by working hard, we're saying Jesus' brutal death was for nothing. Until we accept his gift of grace, we're toiling—needlessly—and worse, we're relegating Jesus' ultimate sacrifice to a mere gesture.

Lord, forgive me for trying to earn a place in heaven. I understand I can never do enough to deserve it. I accept the miracle of grace, and I thank you, Jesus, for accomplishing what I never could. Your death was not for nothing. It was for my life.

You Are Chosen

God decided in advance to adopt us into his own family by bringing us to himself
through Jesus Christ. This is what he wanted to do, and it gave him great pleasure.
EPHESIANS 1:5 NLT

Adopted children never have to wonder if they were wanted. They grow up with the certainty that their parents chose them. What a blessing.

As a child of God, you are granted that same wonderful knowledge. You are his adopted one, chosen specially to bring him pleasure. Not to accomplish any great feat, or to fulfill any grand purpose, but just because he wanted you.

Father, I can't believe you chose me. With all my faults and all the times I go my own way, I'm amazed you call me your beloved child. Knowing I bring pleasure to you—just by being me —is one of the great joys of my life.

He Will Shelter You

He will cover you with his feathers.
He will shelter you with his wings.
His faithful promises are your armor and protection.
PSALM 91:4 NLT

Like an eagle, God shelters us beneath his wings from storms and attacks. The image is powerful, yet also tender. How wonderful it is to be tucked in, right up against him, absorbing his warmth!

Do you rest in this promise of protection, or do you struggle, always poking your head out to see what dangers await? Maybe you've even tried to leave the nest altogether and take care of yourself. If so, return to his side. Accept his protection.

Lord, you are my shelter. Thank you for providing me a safe, warm place to wait out life's storms.
Forgive me for the times I resist you, believing I can do it alone.
Your wings are my armor, and they are mighty to save.

Carry Your Shield

In all circumstances take up the shield of faith,
with which you can extinguish all the flaming darts of the evil one.
EPHESIANS 6:16 ESV

To lose someone in an accident is devastating. To learn it could have been prevented adds immeasurably to the pain. "A seatbelt could have saved her," are heavy words to carry.

As part of the armor of God, the shield of faith allows us to quench flaming arrows—but only if we hold it up. It's our responsibility to hold onto our faith and carry it wherever we go. Setting it down, even briefly, leaves us vulnerable to attack.

Lord, I choose to put on your armor today. I put on your truth, your righteousness, and the glorious news of the gospel, and then I lift and carry the shield of my faith. No flaming arrows will reach me; I will not set my shield aside.

Just Say No

Submit yourselves, then, to God. Resist the devil, and he will flee from you.
JAMES 4:7 NIV

Submit to God; resist the devil. It seems simple, so why do culture—and our own lives—so often say the opposite? How often do we give in to temptation and resist the one leading us to our best life?

Until we surrender our lives to the one who wants only good for us, only peace and light, we are subject to the one who wants to destroy us. He will leave, running scared, but not until we stand with God and tell him "no."

Lord, I come before you today filled with regret for the many times I've chosen dark over light, what is easy over what is right. I want to submit my life to you, but I need your help. Strengthen me, Lord, and help me send the enemy running.

Live at Peace

If it is possible, as far as it depends on you, live at peace with everyone.
ROMANS 12:18 NIV

How does this verse strike you? One extreme, you may think, "Ha! He doesn't know the people in my life." On the other hand, this may be one of the easiest commands in Scripture. You're just that easy-going.

Most of us lie somewhere in the middle. We get along with almost everyone—there's just that one co-worker. And that temperamental middle child. And... live at peace with everyone? We can't control other people, but with Christ's help, we can control our response to them.

Lord, I need your help. When others push my buttons, allow your Spirit to soften me. Make my response loving. Let my words be yours; shine your light through me, bringing peace to our encounter.

Peace and Quiet

The work of righteousness will be peace,
And the eect of righteousness, quietness and assurance forever.

effect

ISAIAH 32:17 NKJV

Peace and quiet. Just saying those words together can bring comfort. It can also bring despair, if they seem out of reach. How, oh how can we claim them?

Through righteousness comes peace, quietness, and assurance. Forever. It's a big word, righteousness, and one you may have shied away from. If so, lean in. Righteousness is not an unattainable ideal of perfection or superiority. It's about putting God first, and living in a way that honors him. In exchange for your honor, he offers the peace and quiet you long for.

Lord, I want to live a righteous life. Not just for the peace you oer in return,

offer

or the quiet assurance of your love for me, but because you are God, wholly deserving of my honor and devotion.

Why?

As you do not know the path of the wind,
or how the body is formed in a mother's womb,
so you cannot understand the work of God,
the Maker of all things.
ECCLESIASTES 11:5 NIV

"Why?" Call to mind a toddler who has just grasped the meaning and power of this wonderful little word. Over and over, to everything they hear, they respond, "Why?"

As we grow we learn to stop asking why so often, but inside our minds, we maintain a powerful desire to know. It is human nature. However, when it comes to the mind of God, we cannot satisfy this desire. His mind—his ways—cannot be known. Accepting and even embracing this truth is a sign of spiritual growth.

Father, I long to know you! Even regarding that which I cannot know, my soul cries out, "But why?" Please help me enjoy the wondering, Lord. Help me rest in your sovereignty.

Coffee with God

I rise before dawn and cry for help;
I wait for Your words.
PSALM 119:147 NASB

How is morning for you? Do you rise before you need to, eager to start your day, or is the snooze button your best friend? If you are in the former group, do you begin your day with God?

Numerous times in Scripture, we are encouraged to be morning people.

For some, this advice is not even necessary; for others, it seems impossibly out of reach. "I'm just not wired that way," we say. Perhaps, if this is us, a rewiring is in order. If you knew you had a coffee date with the Father, would you even need an alarm?

Lord, I don't want to miss a minute with you. Beginning my day in your Word, soaking up your wisdom, is a joy and a privilege. Whether for the first or the thousand and first time, I desire to spend the first minutes of every day alone with you.

Spirited Worship

"God is Spirit, so those who worship him must worship in spirit and in truth."
JOHN 4:24 NLT

How do you define "spirit"? A feisty, hard to break horse is considered spirited. An athlete overcoming great hardship is said to have an indomitable spirit. In both examples, what's being described is something beyond the body. And so it is with the Spirit of God.

We may think we know him the least, but consider this: God the Father and Jesus the Son are in heaven. It is the Holy Spirit intervening in our lives, teaching, comforting, and protecting us. It is the Spirit who is our intimate companion, and he is wholly deserving of our worship.

Holy Spirit of God, until we are together in heaven, I can only guess at the ways you influence and guide the course of my life. How can I express my love and gratitude? I can never worship you enough, but I will worship you all I can.

Real Love

*Since ancient times no one has heard, no ear has perceived,
no eye has seen any God besides you,
who acts on behalf of those who wait for him.*
ISAIAH 64:4 NIV

Authenticity. It matters, doesn't it? We wonder if the gem, the handbag, the promise, is real. We've all heard the expression, "If it's too good to be true, it's probably not," so we scrutinize the people and possessions in our lives, looking for authenticity.

What great comfort we can take in our God: the one, true God! All his promises are true; all his gifts are good. His love is authentic, and it is ours to claim.

*Lord, you are God. The one, the only, the Almighty God. Who am I that you should
act on my behalf, that you should speak into my life? And yet you do.
May my love for you be authentic, may my words of praise be true.*

*F*oolish Ones

"The eyes of the Lord search the whole earth in order to strengthen those whose hearts are fully committed to him. What a fool you have been! From now on you will be at war."
2 CHRONICLES 16:9 NLT

You blew it. Those three words carry a weight none of us wishes to bear, yet at some point we all must. That actions have consequences is a hard, painful truth. Perhaps you are living it now.

Be encouraged. Yes, you will face many trials, but because of Jesus' work on the cross, you need never face them alone.

Father, I am foolish. I know you are all I need, yet I often turn to the world for satisfaction and approval. This weakens me, and distances me from your love and protection. Strengthen me today, Lord, and prepare me for the battles I must face. I give you my heart again and ask you to protect it.

Tell Your Story

> Let the redeemed of the Lord tell their story—
> those he redeemed from the hand of the foe.
>
> PSALM 107:2 NIV

What's your story? Whether it's so complex you barely know where to begin, or you think it's too insignificant to tell, be assured that it matters.

From the beginning, God had you in mind. He planned you out to the tiniest detail. He has loved you forever. The way in which you discovered this beautiful truth, or the way it is currently unfolding, is of great significance. Begin telling it to yourself, and be ready to share it when the time comes.

Lord, when I consider your story, mine seems so small. That you chose me to be a part of it is too wonderful to comprehend. Thank you for my story, Father. May I learn to see it as you do: significant, beautiful, and worthy.

Self-Importance in Disguise

*So humble yourselves under the mighty power of God,
and at the right time he will lift you up in honor.*
1 PETER 5:6 NLT

Traffic jams. Grocery store lines on Saturday mornings. The DMV. Did your heart just quicken? Unless you have a great book to read—or you were born with the proverbial "patience of a saint,"—waiting is, at best, an inconvenience.

Have you ever stopped to wonder why? Pondering patience leads to exploring another uncomfortable concept: humility. We're impatient, but why? Is our time any more important than anyone else's? To God, the answer is an unequivocal "no."

Lord, I confess to impatience, which I know is self-importance in disguise.
Allow me to see others as better than myself and to trust that your timing is always best.
Today and every day, I thank you for your unending patience with me.

Written in Stone

God's truth stands firm like a foundation stone with this inscription: "The Lord knows those who are his," and "All who belong to the Lord must turn away from evil."
2 TIMOTHY 2:19 NLT

Among friends, rules evolve. There are flexible policies: "Monday night is Girls Night"; and there are unbreakable codes of friendship: "If you wouldn't say it to her face, don't say it." That rule, we say, is written in stone.

In his second letter to Timothy, Paul shares an important truth in two parts: First, the Lord knows you as his own. Second, those who are his must turn from sin. This matters, we learn, enough to be written in stone.

Lord, I need your help with this one. I am a sinner, yet I love you and I want to follow you with all my heart. Empower me to turn away from evil. I am yours, Father; be my strength.

Surrender

"Be strong, and let us be courageous for our people and for the cities of our God; and may the Lord do what seems good to him."

1 CHRONICLES 19:13 NRSV

How often do you struggle with God for control of your life, asking for certain outcomes, wanting things to go your way? Is surrender to his plan easy for you or a constant challenge?

In the words of Joab to his army, we find a perfect example of the surrendered life: be strong for those we serve; be courageous for the Kingdom of God, and may the Lord's will be done. Nothing for himself, all for the Master. Oh, that we could achieve such trust and devotion!

Lord, I want to use my strength for your people, my courage to execute your plans. I want to want only what seems good to you. But I am afraid, Father. Grant me the faith of Joab, Lord, that I may surrender to your perfect will.

April

Sing praise to God who reigns above,
the God of all creation,
the God of pow'r, the God of love,
the God of our salvation.
With healing balm my soul is filled
and every faithless murmur stilled:
To God all praise and glory.

The Lord is never far away,
but thru all grief distressing,
an ever present help and stay,
our peace and joy and blessing.
As with a mother's tender hand,
God gently leads the chosen band:
To God all praise and glory.

Sing Praise to God Who Reigns Above
By JOHANN J. SCHÜTZ

A Fool for You

The message of the cross is foolishness to those who are perishing,
but to us who are being saved it is the power of God.
1 CORINTHIANS 1:18 NIV

Got you! We may have fallen for a few pranks in our lives or been at the receiving end of someone's joke. We have all had times where our faith has been ridiculed. In these times, it is good to be reminded that human wisdom is nothing in comparison to God's wisdom.

True wisdom is believing in Jesus Christ and accepting his salvation for your life. This can seem like foolishness to the world, but to you it is access to the power of God. You are wise to have chosen to be a fool for Jesus!

Dear Lord, at times I feel like I don't know how to explain my faith, and it can sound a bit weak when I attempt to. Please help me to remember that some will find your gift of salvation foolish, but others are ready to receive the truth of your sacrifice. Help me to rejoice in my salvation, knowing that in following you, I have found true wisdom.

8

Now I Am Found!

"Rejoice with me; I have found my lost sheep."
LUKE 15:6 NIV

How pleasing it is to find something that we thought we had lost! We rejoice in the small victories of finding a lost receipt, pair of sunglasses, or even that matching sock! There is something in our created nature that tells us loss is something to be grieved and discovery is to be celebrated!

The parable of the lost sheep makes it abundantly clear that Jesus celebrates every life that is found in him. The heavens celebrate your salvation, and though you are one of many, Jesus has gone out of the way to find *you*. Such is his love for his own.

Jesus, I thank you for being my shepherd. I thank you for seeking me out and saving me. I thank you that you rejoice in my salvation. Help me to know my significance in you and to share in your delight each time I hear of the salvation of others.

*B*lotted Out

"I, even I, am He who blots out your transgressions for My own sake;
And I will not remember your sins."

ISAIAH 43:25 NKJV

We are not unlike the Israelites, turning from God's ways time and time again. Yet God was merciful to his beloved people; his love was enough to forget their sins. He didn't just cover them up, he completely removed them.

How incredible to know that God removes our sins and remembers them no more. You have been forgiven, and will continue to be forgiven, because in his love, God will always show you mercy. Let your heart be free from condemnation and walk assuredly in his grace.

Heavenly Father, I confess my sins to you now, those known and unknown.
Help me to believe that you really do blot out the things that I would like to forget too!
I want to walk in the freedom of knowing that I am saved by your grace
and in the confidence that you will always show me mercy.

APRIL 4

Citizens of Heaven

Our citizenship is in heaven,
from which we also eagerly wait for the Savior,
the Lord Jesus Christ.
PHILIPPIANS 3:20 NKJV

How great it is to be reminded of home when we are far from it. Sometimes a familiar voice, smell, or picture is enough to trigger a longing to return to where we belong. Paul reminds believers that we belong in heaven, a place that we were truly made for.

Eternity is in our hearts because we were made for the same glory as Jesus! Heaven is our home. Sometimes we don't long for heaven because we are too focused on our earthly home. We can remind ourselves today that we are citizens of heaven and someday we will be where we truly belong.

Jesus, I want to long for your return. Sometimes I focus too much on my earthly goods and forget that I was made for another home. Help me to love you so much that I can't wait to find my place with you and all the other believers in our eternal home.

A Heart of Compassion

Jesus, when He came out, saw a great multitude and was moved with compassion for them, because they were like sheep not having a shepherd.

MARK 6:34 NKJV

When Jesus saw the crowds, he didn't just see them as a bothersome multitude, he saw them as people with needs. Like sheep without a shepherd, people are lost and they need our help. Sometimes the needs are obvious—like help with a newborn or food for the hungry. Other needs are deeper, like the need to have a friend or be healed from emotional pain.

Jesus has compassion! Because we know this loving Jesus, we can have compassion for others. He is able to provide for your needs and he will give you the strength to help others.

Thank you, Lord, for the compassion that you show me each and every day. Thank you for meeting my needs. I pray you will open my eyes to the needs of others. Show me where you want me to help you in meeting those needs. Give me strength to show compassion.

Sing!

Sing praises to God, sing praises!
Sing praises to our King, sing praises!
For God is the King of all the earth;
Sing praises with understanding.

PSALM 47:6-7 NKJV

We may not all have the voice of an angel, but we can all sing, no matter how good or bad it sounds to us. God created you with a voice and with lips that can praise him for all the good things he has done. He is the king of the earth and the king of our hearts. He will delight in your song of praise, even if he is the only one that appreciates it!

So, sing praises to God. Sing, because you understand his goodness. Sing, because you understand his grace. Sing, because he is worthy!

God, you are the king of all the earth. You have been good to me. You have shown your grace toward me. Teach me to delight in singing your praises. I know you delight in me when I praise you.

Powerful Promises

He did not waver through unbelief regarding the promise of God,
but was strengthened in his faith and gave glory to God,
being fully persuaded that God had power to do what he had promised.
ROMANS 4:20-21 NIV

Abraham and Sarah were aged when they were told that God would give them a child. They had good reason not to believe this as it seemed absurd in the natural sense. Sarah even laughed! Yet Abraham let his belief rest in the power of God.

We serve a God who is more than able to carry out his promises! Abraham was given as an example because he looked beyond the circumstance to the greatness of God. When you have a revelation of the power of God, your faith will be strengthened and you will have confidence in God's promises to you, and to this world.

Almighty God, sometimes I doubt that your promises will be fulfilled—both in my own life and in the world. Please forgive my unbelief and reveal your greatness to me, so that I will be strengthened in my faith and be able to give you the glory.

Everlasting Beauty

Charm is deceitful and beauty is passing,
But a woman who fears the Lord, she shall be praised.
PROVERBS 31:30 NKJV

At some point in our lives we are either going to struggle with jealously of those who are better looking than ourselves, or the fact that our outward beauty is passing. The fact is beauty can consume much of our time.

The Bible, however, honors those with a heart for God. Remember this when you are lamenting your outward appearance. You are praised because your heart toward God and your service to him is beautiful. His grace has produced a beauty in you that will never fade.

Lord, help me to understand the beauty that you have placed within me and to know, without a doubt, that my love for you is what makes me beautiful. Let others recognize the truth in my life and be drawn toward everlasting life that is found in you.

Opened, Lifted, and Loved

The Lord opens the eyes of the blind;
The Lord raises up those who are bowed down;
The Lord loves the righteous.
PSALM 146:8 NASB

Our God loves to restore life to his creation. When Jesus came to earth, he healed many physical needs. Greater than physical healing, Jesus came to restore our spiritual brokenness. He opened eyes to the truth, ministered to the poor in spirit, and restored believers to righteousness.

How blessed you are. He has opened your eyes, he will always lift you up in times of trouble, and he loves you because you have chosen the path of righteousness. Let the God of encouragement and restoration be your strength today.

God, you have opened my eyes to the truth; you have forgiven my sin, and you love me. Some days I have fallen harder than others, and today I need you to once again bring restoration to my body and soul. Thank you for picking me up and encouraging me on the path of righteousness.

Be Teachable

Instruct the wise and they will be wiser still;
teach the righteous and they will add to their learning.

PROVERBS 9:9 NIV

The writer of these words knew that a wise person is not just one who has a lot of knowledge. The wise listen to instruction; they continue to seek out wise ways. In the same way, the righteous want to add to the truth they already know.

Is your heart open to receive instruction? Do you want to add to your knowledge of the truth of God's Word? God delights in your pursuit of him and he will instruct and teach you to be wiser still!

Dear Lord, show me when my heart has not been willing to receive your instruction.
I want to know more about you, and I want to hear your truth for my life.
Give me an open heart, mind, and soul to receive wisdom that can only come from you.

Peace Seeds

The seed whose fruit is righteousness is sown in peace by those who make peace.
JAMES 3:18 NASB

Peaceful ways give birth to righteousness. There are times when conflict cannot be avoided, but assuming the role of the peacemaker is often far better than getting your own way. To be a peacemaker requires humility and the desire for the greater good.

One of the many names of Jesus is the Prince of Peace. He is our best example of what it means to sow peace and to make peace. He lives in you, and by drawing on him, you will experience peace in times of trouble and conflict.

God, your Word says that you are the author of peace. Bring peace to my situations, peace in my decisions, and peace in my heart. Help me to become a peacemaker so the fruit I bear in my life will be that of righteousness.

A Very Good Creation

God saw everything that He had made, and indeed it was very good.
GENESIS 1:31 NKJV

On the sixth day, after all other created things, God made man and woman. He made us in his image. On that day he declared that his creation was *very* good. How reassuring it is to know that God's creation was intentionally good. He did not create mistakes or flaws; he created us according to his perfect plan.

The next time you find yourself despairing about all the things that have gone wrong in this world, go back to the beginning. He created all things good. Yes, sin has taken us a long way from this goodness, but God's plan isn't finished yet; he is coming to restore his creation and it will once again be *very* good!

Thank you, God, for your very good creation. Sometimes it is hard to see all of the evil in the world and feel like anything is really good. Help me see beyond this life, to the time when you will restore your creation to perfection.

*N*o More Pain

He will wipe away every tear from their eyes, and death shall be no more, neither shall there be mourning, nor crying, nor pain anymore, for the former things have passed away.

REVELATION 21:4 ESV

We are promised a time when there will be no more pain. This life is full of hardship, but we can live in hope that a day will come where joy will reign supreme!

It is this hope that carries us through the hard times, when we trust that God is still good and that he has good plans for us now and in the future. Rejoice in eternal life, for this is not where it ends!

Lord, I look forward to an eternity of joy, where the pain of this life will be no more. Thank you that even today you can bring relief to my physical pain, healing to my emotional pain, and restoration to my spiritual weakness. Help me to lean on you through the hard times.

Brave Heart

"Have I not commanded you? Be strong and courageous!
Do not tremble or be dismayed, for the Lord your God is with you wherever you go."
JOSHUA 1:9 NASB

Joshua had a big task ahead of him: to lead the entire nation of Israel into the Promised Land. This required defeating great opposition. God reassured Joshua many times with these words, "Be strong and courageous." When God calls his people to do his will, he empowers them with the ability to do it.

You are called of God and are able to do his work because he is with you wherever you go. You are not expected to walk in your own strength. This is why God instructs us to have courage. Our God is a mighty God and we can do all things through him.

Lord, you are worthy of all praise because you alone are above all things. Thank you that you promise to be with me wherever I go. Help me to have courage when the task that you have set before me seems too big or too difficult. I can do all things through you.

Mere Mortals

In God, whose word I praise—
in God I trust and am not afraid.
What can mere mortals do to me?
PSALM 56:4 NIV

"In God We Trust." This is still printed on US currency today, despite many people not truly trusting or believing in God. As Christians, we claim to trust God too. Is this a motto that is written on the currency of your heart—one that you can hold fast to in times when all else seems against you?

We are not always spared harm or hurt, but God is always present and promises to take care of us. It is important to remember that no matter what we face, no "mere mortal" can ever take away our eternal destiny in Jesus.

Jesus, I praise you, and I trust that you are taking care of my life. Sometimes I need to be reminded that ultimately my life is in your hands, and that you are the author that determines its course. Let my motto always be, "In God I trust."

Practice Produces Peace

Keep on doing the things that you have learned and received and heard and seen in me, and the God of peace will be with you.

PHILIPPIANS 4:9 NRSV

Paul was chosen by God to carry the good news of Jesus Christ to all who were willing to receive it. His messages to the believers guided them in the truth about Jesus and how to live a righteous life.

We have been blessed to have all of this truth available to us through the Bible.

But we need to be more than just good readers or listeners. We are encouraged to keep practicing the things that we have learned through God's Word. When we put the truth into action, we are rewarded with the knowledge of the presence of God near to us.

Lord, help me to read your Word with the intent of putting what I receive into practice. Forgive me when I have only been a hearer of your Word, and not a doer. Let my life be an example to others, and as I obey your Word, grant me the peace of knowing you are with me.

Church Siblings

He has given us this command: Anyone who loves God must also love their brother and sister.
1 JOHN 4:21 NIV

Family members can be some of the hardest people to get along with! In the same way, people within our church or community of believers are not always easy to show love to.

We cannot separate our love for God from our love for others. When we love God, we obey his commands and he desires that we have right relationships with each other. Be encouraged that you have been given a family of brothers and sisters in Christ, and they are there to love you as you choose to love them.

Dear God, thank you for the community of believers that you have placed me in.
Help me to show them love as I would show love to any of my brothers or sisters.
Help me to continue to remember that we are all one family in you.

Starry Host

You alone are the Lord. You made the heavens, even the highest heavens, and all their starry host, the earth and all that is on it, the seas and all that is in them. You give life to everything, and the multitudes of heaven worship you.

NEHEMIAH 9:6 NIV

It is amazing enough that the Lord made the earth and everything in it, from the blade of grass to the complexities of conception. Even more amazing is that he created the heavens, the universe, and everything beyond it. There are created things that we will not get to see or understand while we are limited by our earthly bodies and knowledge.

God gave life to everything that he created. It is not only on earth that we worship God. He is worshipped in all creation. What an amazing God we serve; he is worthy of our praise.

God, I thank you for showing yourself through creation. Thank you that I get to enjoy your good creation and that even though I don't understand the extent of what you have made, I am in awe of your greatness. Be Lord of my life, as you are Lord of all creation.

On Your Behalf

He is able to save completely those who come to God through him,
because he always lives to intercede for them.

HEBREWS 7:25 NIV

When Jesus died on the cross and rose again, he not only took the penalty for our sin, he also became the way in which we can approach God boldly. He made us holy.

It is only through Jesus that we are saved, and the Bible said that he is always interceding for us—past, present, and future. How encouraging to know that we have someone who stands on our behalf to declare us holy and righteous.

Dear Jesus, thank you so much for suffering the cross so that I could be completely saved and made holy before God. Thank you for interceding for me so I can live a life that is full of your grace for me.

*D*ebt of Love

Let no debt remain outstanding, except the continuing debt to love one another,
for whoever loves others has fulfilled the law.

ROMANS 13:8 NIV

When a bill arrives in the mail, we are reminded that we owe money in return for something that has been done for us. If we leave it for too long, it can cause anxiety and even resentment on both sides. This is one reason the Scripture reminds us not to leave a debt outstanding.

However, the Bible instructs us to treat love as debt, in the sense that we should continually be compelled to love one another and to give love even if it has not been earned! This is the extreme love that God has shown us. Let his unending and unconditional love for you be the reminder letter that you need to spur you on to love others in the same way.

Jesus, you continue to amaze me with the love that you have for me.
I know that I don't need to earn your love and that you will never give up on me.
Remind me, Holy Spirit, to continue to love others in this way.

His Riches

This same God who takes care of me will supply all your needs from his glorious riches,
which have been given to us in Christ Jesus.

PHILIPPIANS 4:19 NLT

The Lord's riches are found in his goodness, his grace, and his sovereignty as king over all. God is always able to provide for all of our needs. Sometimes we may feel as though we are not worthy to receive from the Lord. Sometimes we find it hard to trust and we worry about our needs.

The good news of Jesus Christ is that he has given us access to the throne of God. You are a child of the king and he offers his riches to you. All you need to do is love him, ask him, and trust in his goodness. His promise is to take care of you.

Almighty God, you are sovereign and good. Thank you that you want to take care of me.
There are things that I feel I need right now and I submit them to you.
I pray you would take the burden from me as I continue to trust you each and every day.

Water Ways

*Let justice flow like a river,
and let goodness flow like a never-ending stream.*
AMOS 5:24 NCV

We all have a sense of needing to keep things fair, that's why we have referees at sports matches, lines at the store, and a judge at a court case. When we see or experience injustice, we long for it to be made right.

We know that God is just and that he also anguishes over injustice. What a blessing to him when his people do what is right—when we treat people fairly and continually do good. Be encouraged that as you pursue righteousness, his goodness to you will be a refreshing stream that will never dry up.

Lord, you are fair and merciful. I know that there is injustice in this imperfect life, so I look forward to the day when you will put everything right. Until then, allow me to be like flowing waters of goodness to others as I seek to live a life of righteousness.

Continue in Christ

Just as you received Christ Jesus as Lord, continue to live your lives in him, rooted and built up in him, strengthened in the faith as you were taught, and overflowing with thankfulness.

COLOSSIANS 2:6-7 NIV

Receiving Christ causes a wonderful transformation. But there is fullness to the Christian life that goes beyond salvation. The Scripture says that we *continue* our lives in him. This means that every day we have the opportunity to grow in our relationship with God.

As we develop our relationship with Christ, we experience a deep assurance of our faith and we are empowered to live a full life. It is easy to be thankful for all of the good things Jesus is doing in your life as you grow from strength to strength.

Lord Jesus, thank you for what I have been learning through your holy Scriptures. Remind me to continue in my faith by following your example and listening to your voice. I am so thankful for my salvation and I am even more thankful that you choose to be in relationship with me.

Lean on the Lord

Trust in the Lord with all your heart,
And lean not on your own understanding.
PROVERBS 3:5 NKJV

When we are faced with challenging situations, particularly when we are making big decisions, we often try to figure things out on our own. When that doesn't work, we start to pray. There's nothing wrong with this, but wouldn't it be better if we left it up to God in the first place?

God knows us intimately, and he knows our life situations. When we lean on God in times of need, the burden of trying to understand things in our own minds can be shifted to trusting in our hearts that God will work it out.

Lord, there have been big decisions in my life that I wish I had trusted you more with. I know that I can trust you and that you will help me, even if it is in a way that I don't expect or even understand! I give my heart to you and place my life in your hands.

Walking in Works

We are His workmanship, created in Christ Jesus for good works,
which God prepared beforehand so that we would walk in them.

EPHESIANS 2:10 NASB

God has always had a plan for your life. He created, designed, and brought you into being. He has gifted you with talents, nurtured you, and developed character in you as you have matured. You are his wonderful workmanship!

God knew from the beginning how to uniquely design you to empower you to do good works. Best of all, he created you in Christ Jesus, whose redemption and healing on the cross gave you all the grace that you need to walk in his ways.

Dear Jesus, thank you for sacrificing your life on the cross so that I can walk in grace and carry out the good works that you designed me for. Thank you that it is not my strength but your strength within me that helps me each and every day.

Satisfied

Because your love is better than life, my lips will glorify you.
I will praise you as long as I live, and in your name I will lift up my hands.
I will be fully satisfied as with the richest of foods; with singing lips my mouth will praise you.

PSALM 63:3-5 NIV

There are times in our lives when we really need answers or a breakthrough, and sometimes we just want to be blessed. Our loving Father says to simply ask.

God wants to give us good gifts. You might not want to ask for things because you feel they are too much, or too specific. But God is able to handle our requests—he won't give us things that will bring us harm or that we will use for our selfish gain. He knows what is best for us. His love is better than life itself, and he knows exactly how to satisfy us.

Lord, there are many things that I need and many things I want. I ask you for them now because I know that you are a loving Father who wants to answer me today.

Holy Spirit Words

"When you are brought into the synagogues before the leaders and other powerful people, don't worry about how to defend yourself or what to say. At that time the Holy Spirit will teach you what you must say."

LUKE 12:11-12 NCV

Defending our faith has always been a challenge. We might not be dragged into a court over our beliefs as some were in the apostle Paul's time, but we can expect to have opposition and confrontation about our faith.

The Holy Spirit was given to us as a helper. He fills us and reminds us of the words of Jesus. He brings Scripture to our mind. In those times when you need to defend the gospel of Jesus Christ, be confident that the Holy Spirit will give you the right words.

Holy Spirit, I thank you that you dwell within me. Teach me what to say when I feel challenged to share or defend my faith in you. I believe in your power to bring your words to my lips as I speak.

From East to West

If I rise with the sun in the east and settle in the west beyond the sea,
even there you would guide me. With your right hand you would hold me.
PSALM 139:9-10 NCV

Moving on from anywhere can be disconcerting. A new circumstance, house, or even country means that we have to leave what we have been comfortable with and step out into the unknown.

Take courage that no matter where you go, the Lord will always go with you. He is as far east as the rising sun, and as far west as the sunset. He will guide you as you move, and he will hold you when you get there.

Lord, this world is small in comparison to your presence. You promise to be with me wherever I go. Guide me in the next step of my life; give me confidence to move to where you have called me to be. I trust in you from the rising of the sun to its going down.

Assignment from Jesus

My life is worth nothing to me unless I use it for finishing the work assigned me by the Lord Jesus—the work of telling others the Good News about the wonderful grace of God.

ACTS 20:24 NLT

When it is all said and done, there is nothing more important in our lives than the good news of Jesus. He came to earth to reveal God's nature. He sacrificed his life to save us from our sin. He defeated death once and for all. He gave us a life of grace that we might walk in freedom. We have a lot of good news to share!

The joy of knowing good news is in being able to share it. Instead of spending your life trying to figure out exactly what you are supposed to be doing, remember the assignment that Jesus has given you—to tell others about his grace. This is an assignment worth finishing!

Dear Jesus, thank you for all that you have done for me. Help me to remember what is most important in this life. Give me the grace and boldness to share your good news with those around me.

*W*hole Restoration

My whole being, praise the Lord and do not forget all his kindnesses.
He forgives all my sins and heals all my diseases.
PSALM 103:2-3 NCV

Our God is a God of restoration. He shows us his kindness, through his love, in that he cares for our entire being. Not only does God want to restore a right relationship with you, he also wants to restore your body to health.

When we are spiritually or physically weak, we can sometimes forget the promises of God. In these times, think on his character; remember that he is a loving Father who wants the best for you. Praise him with all of your heart, soul, and mind, and watch him bring restoration to the areas of your life that need it the most.

Heavenly Father, I praise you with my whole being. I remember your kindness toward me, and I ask you to show me your mercy. Forgive my sins and renew my heart. Heal my body and restore my health.

May

Cast thy burden on the Lord,
Only lean upon His word;
Thou wilt soon have cause to bless
His eternal faithfulness.

Ever in the raging storm
Thou shalt see His cheering form,
Hear His pledge of coming aid:
"It is I, be not afraid."

He will gird thee by His pow'r,
In thy weary fainting hour;
Lean then, loving, on His word;
Cast thy burden on the Lord.

Cast Thy Burden on the Lord
By John Cennick & George Rawson

Equipped for Battle

Put on the full armor of God, so that you can take your stand against the devil's schemes.
EPHESIANS 6:11 NIV

At times it is hard to acknowledge that we are in a spiritual battle and that there is opposition to the good works of God. The devil does have his schemes, but God has provided us with everything we need to equip ourselves against these schemes.

We have the truth in the person of Jesus Christ. We have been granted salvation and righteousness through his grace. We have peace in the confidence of our eternal destiny. God's Word brings life. This is the armor that you can equip yourself with daily to be able to stand firm in your faith. Be strengthened!

Lord Jesus, thank you for providing me with everything I need to stand firm in my faith. This life can get hard for me at times and I pray that you would remind me to face my struggles with your truth, righteousness, and peace. Help me to always use your Word to equip me for battle.

Any Prayer Counts

Pray in the Spirit on all occasions with all kinds of prayers and requests.
EPHESIANS 6:18 NIV

Often we are too analytical with our prayers. We think we ought to make them sound fancy or humble. We can treat prayer like money: we don't want to spend it on the wrong things. We might not be able to trust our intentions when we pray, but God sees our heart.

The Lord wants you to talk with him in all occasions and with all kinds of prayers. Sometimes our prayer is a quick cry for help, and sometimes it is an hour-long worship session! No matter what kind of prayer, Jesus will always be present to hear you.

Jesus, I don't always know how to pray, how short or how informal I can be, or what things are acceptable to pray for. I thank you for reminding me that it doesn't actually matter. What matters is that I open my heart to you at all times and acknowledge that I need you in any and every area of my life.

Chased by Grace

Surely goodness and mercy shall follow me
All the days of my life;
And I will dwell in the house of the Lord Forever.
PSALM 23:6 NKJV

We leave footprints as we walk along the journey of life. Some of these footprints are left from walking in the dirt and they need to be cleaned up because they don't belong to the path of righteousness.

God wants to lead you in the right direction. As you live in his ways your path will be followed by goodness, and his mercy will clean up those footsteps that have gone in the wrong direction. His grace will follow you all of your life. It is by this grace that you will dwell in the house of the Lord forever!

Heavenly Father, I want to dwell in your house forever. I trust in your goodness and mercy to follow me as I journey through life with you before me, behind me, and beside me. Allow me to know your presence today.

Spiritual Guidance

If we live by the Spirit, let us also be guided by the Spirit.

GALATIANS 5:25 NRSV

Living by the Spirit means that we are continually dying to the sinful desires of our fallen nature. When we surrender our sinful nature to the cross, we produce fruit that is proof of the Spirit working within us. We see love, joy, peace, patience, kindness, goodness, faithfulness, gentleness, and self-control.

Not only can we see these fruits when we are living by the Spirit, but we can also use them to guide us in the right way. You will bring life into your situations and relationships when you give preference to the way of the Spirit.

Holy Spirit, guide me as I try to live by the Spirit. Forgive me when I display selfishness and gratify the desires of the flesh. I know that I am going to have to surrender to your ways on a daily basis, so I surrender all of my selfish ambition today and ask that others will see your fruit working within me.

Key to Success

My child, do not forget my teaching, but keep my commands in mind.
Then you will live a long time, and your life will be successful.
PROVERBS 3:1-2 NCV

Today success is associated with riches and social status. Often, successful people have also had an academic advantage, having had access to good teachers and successful strategies to learning well.

In the same way, we are able to pursue Godly success through Godly wisdom and teaching. The teachings of Jesus are profound and life giving. We have an advantage in that the wisdom of God and his commands have been written down for us so we cannot forget. Study his Word and commit his teaching to memory, and you will have all that you need to live a full life in God!

Lord God, teach me your ways. Remind me to read your Word and give me strategies to remember the Scriptures. I recognize that I may never have worldly success, but I know that I can achieve Godly success by remembering your teaching and keeping your commands.

A Patient Promise

The Lord is not slow about His promise, as some count slowness, but is patient toward you, not wishing for any to perish but for all to come to repentance.
2 PETER 3:9 NASB

Jesus will return one day—he promised he would! Until then, however, we live in the "in-between." The kingdom has come, but not in its fullness, and we await the time when the earth and everything in it will be restored.

Jesus' return can seem slow to those of us who are waiting, but if we understand the love that Jesus has for humanity, we can understand, in part, his timing for waiting for others to reach repentance. Praise Jesus for his love, and be patient in his promise. He will return!

Jesus, I don't fully understand your way and why some of the promises that I read about in your Word have not been fulfilled. Give me a holy patience, one that understands your heart for the world. Grant me that same heart for those who don't know you yet. Lead us all to repentance.

Pentecost Power

"You shall receive power when the Holy Spirit has come upon you; and you shall be witnesses to Me in Jerusalem, and in all Judea and Samaria, and to the end of the earth."

ACTS 1:8 NKJV

The Holy Spirit can be a powerful influence in your life if you learn how to hear his voice. When the Holy Spirit came on the early church believers, they witnessed many miracles, including being able to hear each other speaking in other languages! Many people became Christians as a result of these Holy Spirit moments!

When you genuinely display the power of the Holy Spirit, people will be drawn to you and your witness of the gospel of Jesus Christ. Be encouraged that the same Spirit that came upon the believers on that day is with you today.

Holy Spirit, I want to receive your power in this moment. Let your presence be so evident in my life that others recognize something different about me. Give me the boldness to testify that the joy and peace that I experience is because of your grace in my life. Let your gospel reach the ends of the earth.

Humble Highs

Humble yourselves before the Lord, and he will lift you up.
JAMES 4:10 NIV

It seems an upside down thing to say—that in humility, rather than pride, you will be lifted up. Usually humility comes with a sense of shame. There is no shame, however, in humility before God. The Lord loves humility because it draws you close to him and allows him to work through you without having to battle your pride.

Humility before the Lord is the acknowledgement that you need his forgiveness, his grace, and his strength in all areas and at all times in your life. In your humility before him, he will encourage you, strengthen you, and lift you up!

Lord, I am sorry when my pride gets in the way of you speaking and working in my life. I humble myself before you now and ask for your grace and your strength in all areas of my life. Thank you for lifting me up.

Free of the Past

If anyone is in Christ, he is a new creation; old things have passed away;
behold, all things have become new.
2 CORINTHIANS 5:17 NKJV

Before Christ, we were slaves to our sinful nature and had no freedom from the things we had done wrong. When Jesus Christ died on the cross, he took our sin upon himself. When he rose again, he displayed his victory over sin and death.

Your sins of the past belong to the old person, the one that did not have Christ. As Christians, we live by grace and in the forgiveness that God grants us because of Jesus' sacrifice. Live as the new creation God has made you to be, walking in the freedom of his grace.

Dear Jesus, thank you for sacrificing your life so I can be free from sin.
Help me to avoid the temptation to revert back to the old person that I was.
Thank you that all of those things have passed away, and that you have made me new.

Strength of My Heart

Whom have I in heaven but you? And earth has nothing I desire besides you.
My flesh and my heart may fail, but God is the strength of my heart
and my portion forever.

PSALM 73:25-26 NIV

When God said, "I am," he declared how all-encompassing his presence is, both in heaven and on earth. When we begin to understand both the love and the greatness of our God, we become convinced that he is everything.

The Lord is your all; there is nothing in heaven and earth that is greater. His love for you will give you everything you need. While everything else around you may fail and fall away, the knowledge of God will forever rest in your heart. He is your portion, forever.

Holy God, you are the reason for all life, for my life, and for eternal life. Thank you that your love is enough to sustain my heart. My body may fail me, and my words may never be able to express my gratefulness to you, but you are more than enough for me both in this life and in the life to come.

Convinced of Love

I am convinced that neither death, nor life, nor angels, nor rulers, nor things present, nor things to come, nor powers, nor height, nor depth, nor anything else in all creation, will be able to separate us from the love of God in Christ Jesus our Lord.
ROMANS 8:38-39 NRSV

Our relationship with Jesus Christ is eternal. You may have just begun this journey with him, or have been a friend of God for all of your life. Whatever your life story, you are covered by his grace and can never be separated from his love.

Jesus Christ is all about love for his people. He humbled himself and took on human form for you. He suffered rejection for you. He took himself to the cross and died for you. Nothing would have stopped his love for you. His love will surround you in the highest height and the deepest depth. Be convinced that nothing will separate you from the love you have found in Jesus.

Jesus, thank you for everything you have endured for me. Thank you for showing me love by sacrificing your life for me. I acknowledge that I may never fully understand the love that you have for me, but I am convinced that nothing will separate me from your love.

Opportunity for Joy

When troubles of any kind come your way, consider it an opportunity for great joy.
For you know that when your faith is tested, your endurance has a chance to grow.
JAMES 1:2-3 NLT

It's not easy to approach troubles with joy, unless we can understand how these things work out for good. One of the best things that comes from trouble is that we are tested. And while testing seems like something to get anxious about, when we pass, we have more confidence than we had before.

Endurance is a quality that is crucial to staying true to our faith in the hard times. Rather than giving up when troubles come, hold onto your faith in Jesus and ask the Holy Spirit to help you in times of trouble.

Lord, there have been times lately where I feel that my faith is really being tested.
Help me to consider my misfortunes as an opportunity to lean on you and develop my endurance.
Give me joy in the middle of my trouble, knowing that better things are coming.

Quenched

The desert and the parched land will be glad;
the wilderness will rejoice and blossom.
ISAIAH 35:1 NIV

There are times in life when we feel like we are always striving and never getting anywhere; where we thirst for something more but still feel dry. God has promised that there will be a day when we, the redeemed, will no longer thirst for fulfillment; when everything we desire will be satisfied.

Before that day, however, God is still willing and able to grant you an oasis in the desert and give you signs of life in whatever kind of "wilderness" you may be experiencing. Just like the promise Jesus made to the woman at the well, the water that he gives is everlasting and becomes in us a spring of water welling up to eternal life.

God, thank you for the water that you give to satisfy my soul. I want to draw from your everlasting well so that I can endure the desert moments and experience growth in the times of wilderness.

Provision for the Generous

Now may He who supplies seed to the sower, and bread for food,
supply and multiply the seed you have sown and increase the fruits of your righteousness.
2 CORINTHIANS 9:10 NKJV

The beginning of generosity is provision. Just as a farmer requires seed for a harvest, we must also be provided with something to sow. God has supplied you with everything you need to help in growing his kingdom. He will increase your resources as you diligently plant the seeds of faith.

As God multiplies your resources, he will also increase the harvest, that is, the good that comes from what you have sown. He gives to you generously that you might be generous. Be encouraged to give from what he has given you, and watch the blessings in your life increase.

Heavenly Father, you continue to supply me with all that I need. Help me to sow my seeds of faith so that I might see growth in my life and in the lives of others. Lead me to generosity so that your work will be done on earth as it is in heaven.

Light of the Dawn

Even in darkness light dawns for the upright,
for those who are gracious and compassionate and righteous.
PSALM 112:4 NIV

The middle of the night can be an anxious time to be awake, often bringing irrational fears of danger, disturbing thoughts, or a disquieted spirit. In contrast, the first rays of light in the morning can bring one peace, hope, and joy.

Life does not always seem full of hope and joy, especially when you have experienced hurt, anxiety, or depression. God's truth, however, is that even in your moments of darkness his light will dawn for you. Grace, compassion, and righteousness belong to you as you allow Jesus to shine his life into your heart.

Jesus, sometimes I despair over the darkness in this world. In these times, I choose to trust in the light that you bring into my life and into the world. Let me experience the hope and joy that comes with the dawn.

Heavenly Scent

Thanks be to God who always leads us in triumph in Christ,
and through us diffuses the fragrance of His knowledge in every place.
2 CORINTHIANS 2:14 NKJV

In ancient Rome, a triumph was a ceremonious procession granted to generals who had won a decisive victory in battle. Jesus Christ has triumphed over sin and death and we are called to be a part of this victory! He has led us in battle and we are on the winning side!

The victory of Jesus can be displayed in our words and actions, but it is also described as a perfume that diffuses into every place that we go. When you carry the confidence of your triumph, it will sit in the air around you and cause others to detect the fragrance of Jesus.

Thank you, Jesus, for winning the battle over sin and letting me follow you in this victory. I pray that you would give me the strength to overcome temptation and to lead a life of triumph. Let your spirit in me be as a lovely perfume to those you bring into my life.

Thunder Theology

"God's voice thunders in marvelous ways;
he does great things beyond our understanding."
JOB 37:5 NIV

Thunder is powerful, mysterious, and commanding. It's little wonder that God's voice is described in this way. With his voice, he created the heavens and the earth. His voice can command all things into submission to his will.

Throughout history God has done great things, and he is able to do great things today. What are the great things that you have been asking for in your life? Do you believe that he can do them? Just like the thunder, we may not fully comprehend how God works, but we know that he is present and powerful. Trust him to do great things.

Almighty God, you created the heavens and the earth. You are powerful and worthy of my praise.
Thank you for doing great things in my life and in the world around me.
Teach me to worship you as the awesome God that you are.

Believing Is Not Seeing!

These things I have written to you who believe in the name of the Son of God, that you may know that you have eternal life, and that you may continue to believe in the name of the Son of God.

1 JOHN 5:13 NKJV

When Jesus came to earth, there were many who saw him and witnessed his teaching and miracles, and yet did not believe. It is incredible that the belief in Jesus has carried on, long after he was taken back into heaven.

Jesus calls blessed those who have not seen him and yet believe. You are blessed because you love him and have faith in him. This is why you can have joy in the midst of all situations—because you have faith in the truth, and it will one day bring you to glory.

Lord Jesus, I have not physically seen you, but I know that you are there. You have sent your Holy Spirit to help me have faith in you as the Son of God and the Savior of my life. Give me joy as I glorify you in my heart and in my deeds.

Fixed on Him

Looking to Jesus, the founder and perfecter of our faith, who for the joy that was set before him endured the cross, despising the shame, and is seated at the right hand of the throne of God.

HEBREWS 12:2 ESV

It is hard to imagine how Jesus endured such overwhelming suffering on the cross, but the Scripture explains that he looked towards the joy set before him. Jesus saw beyond his suffering for the purpose of our redemption, and he knew that God would be glorified.

In the same way, we are urged to look to Jesus. Some translations say that we "fix our eyes" on Jesus. This means that even when you are going through troubles of your own, you can focus on Jesus. Keeping our eyes on him allows us to see beyond our suffering and to know that God will ultimately be glorified as we keep our faith in him.

Jesus, you are the beginning and the end, and today I choose to fix my eyes on you so that I can see beyond my troubles and suffering. I know that you are now seated at the right hand of God and I desire to glorify you.

The Eternal Kingdom

Since we are receiving a Kingdom that is unshakable,
let us be thankful and please God by worshiping him with holy fear and awe.
HEBREWS 12:28 NLT

Kings and queens hold their throne for a time, but ultimately their reign ends, either through defeat or death. The kingdom of God is not like the kingdom of men. It is undefeatable and unshakeable.

You belong to God's kingdom, and it will never be defeated. His power will not be surpassed by any other principality or power. Be thankful that you belong to this kingdom. Worship God as the king of this universe and the king of your heart!

Lord, you are my king and I honor and adore you. Help me to remember that your kingdom has the authority over all, and that it will not be defeated. Even though you are a great and awesome king, you love me as a daughter. Teach me to worship you in reverence and love.

Fiery Furnace

> "If we are thrown into the blazing furnace, the God whom we serve is able to save us.
> He will rescue us from your power, Your Majesty."
>
> DANIEL 3:17 NLT

What confidence Shadrach, Meshach, and Abednego had in God's power to rescue them from the blazing furnace! Not only did they refuse to worship the king's idol, they willingly went through the fire to prove the power of their God.

You are unlikely to have to go through literal flames for God, but he will honor your decision to stand up for your faith in him. You may feel pressured by the majority to live a certain way, to accept other religions, and to compromise your standards. Be encouraged that our God is the God who miraculously saved these faithful men from the fire, and he is the only one worthy of praise.

Dear God, give me faith as strong as these three men. Help me to stand against the idols of this world and to hold fast to my belief in you. I want to serve you for the rest of my days, and I ask for your protection along the way.

Evergreen

Blessed are those who trust in the Lord, whose trust is the Lord.
They shall be like a tree planted by water, sending out its roots by the stream.
It shall not fear when heat comes, and its leaves shall stay green;
in the year of drought it is not anxious, and it does not cease to bear fruit.

JEREMIAH 17:7-8 NRSV

Trees that are planted closest to the source of life are strong, healthy, and fruitful. In contrast, a tree that is not planted near water will struggle to survive when the heat or drought comes.

The Lord is your source of life! You will draw close to God as you pray, worship, read his Word, and fellowship with other believers. These are the roots you send out; they allow you to deepen your relationship with God. When you know you are close to the source, you will have confidence that through heat or drought, his refreshing waters are always available to sustain and bless you.

Lord God, I choose to draw close to you now in prayer, knowing that as I communicate with you,
I am able to draw from your strength. Let me continually plant myself close to you,
for my trust is in you.

My Redeemer Lives

"I know that my Redeemer lives,
and at the last he will stand upon the earth."
JOB 19:25 ESV

If you are familiar with the story of Job, you will know that God allowed him to suffer greatly; he lost his family, his health, and his wealth. We can empathize with Job as he wrestled with his understanding of God and the futility of life.

In the middle of suffering, the only thing that we may be able to hold on to is a declaration. While Job could not comprehend his suffering or God's ways, he knew in his heart and declared with his lips, "My Redeemer lives." Be uplifted as you dwell on that declaration. God is the one that ultimately has the final say for your life and for this earth, and you can boldly claim that he lives!

Lord God, thank you for the men and women who walked on this earth before us, who demonstrated astounding faith in the midst of suffering. I declare now, Lord, throughout the troubles of life, that my Redeemer lives!

Always Helping

God is not unjust; he will not forget your work and the love you have shown him as you have helped his people and continue to help them.

HEBREWS 6:10 NIV

Do you sometimes feel as though you give and give and are never appreciated? Women seem to have a natural tendency to help and care for those in need. Sometimes, though, this love towards others seems to go unrecognized and it can almost make us feel resentful.

While people may not take the time to appreciate your help, God most certainly will! He does not forget that you have shown love to his people, and he knows that this equates to your love for him. Keep up the good work!

Father God, I have felt unappreciated at times for the love that I have given others. Thank you that you notice even when others don't. Allow me to remember that it is more important to please you than it is to please others. Strengthen me to continue the good work.

He Rejoices over You

The Lord your God in your midst, The Mighty One, will save;
He will rejoice over you with gladness, He will quiet you with His love,
He will rejoice over you with singing.
ZEPHANIAH 3:17 NKJV

Parents are usually insanely proud of their children. It doesn't seem to matter what particular gift a child might have, a parent will always find something in that child to praise. A parent's love is not about what the child can do, but about who they are. They see a beautiful heart and amazing potential.

Our heavenly Father feels like this about us—only much more. Not only is he always present, he's protective, proud, and loving. Can you imagine him today, being so happy to be near you that he sings and rejoices over you! You are his daughter, and you are loved.

Father, sometimes I forget that you love me for who I am, not what I do. You see my heart and you rejoice over me. Give me the confidence to walk through life with the knowledge that I have a heavenly Father who delights in me so much that he can't help but sing!

The Many Wonders of God

Many, O Lord my God, are the wonders you have done.
The things you planned for us. None can compare with you;
were I to speak and tell of your deeds, they would be too many to declare.
PSALM 40:5 NIV

It is good to give God the glory for all the things that are too wonderful for words. We know from the Bible that God has acted powerfully on many occasions to preserve his chosen people. We know that Jesus performed spectacular miracles. The Holy Spirit moved mightily on the early church and still shows his power today.

God didn't stop at making the earth; he continues to make wonderful things in this life. You can probably think of many examples of how God has done great things for you. Imagine how many believers can tell these stories as well… there are too many to declare!

Lord God, I thank you for all the wonderful plans you have in store for my life. You are too great for words, and I simply declare that you are awesome!

Thirsty for Mercy

Come, all you who are thirsty, come to the waters;
and you who have no money, come, buy and eat!
Come, buy wine and milk without money and without cost.
ISAIAH 55:1 NIV

Money is used for what we want, but mostly for the things that we need—like food and even water. Imagine walking into a grocery store and being offered anything you want without having to pay a cent! This is a picture of the mercy that Jesus has shown all of us through his sacrifice.

We need God's mercy in the same way that we thirst for water. Wine and milk were expensive items in the time this was written, and to offer these free of charge would have been a great sacrifice. What Christ did for you on the cross came at a great price, but it was all because of his great love for you.

Dear Lord Jesus, I come to you as a thirsty child in need of your mercy.
Thank you that you have paid the price for me to receive your forgiveness.
I am thankful for the grace that you have freely given me.

Divine Decisions

Oh, how great are God's riches and wisdom and knowledge!
How impossible it is for us to understand his decisions and his ways!

ROMANS 11:33 NLT

How do you know when you have made the right decision? When we are faced with uncertainty in a significant choice, we use a variety of strategies to come up with the right answer. Some of them are good reasoning, and others are not!

We should be careful not to project our decision-making difficulties onto the way the Lord makes decisions. The Bible says that his ways are not our ways and his thoughts are not our thoughts. God is rich with wisdom and knowledge; therefore, his ways are extremely superior to ours. Let him into your decision making process and trust his ways!

Lord you have wisdom and knowledge well beyond my understanding. I lay my decisions before you and ask for your guidance. I don't always understand why things happen the way they do, but I trust that your decisions are always best.

Contentment in All Circumstances

I know what it is to be in need, and I know what it is to have plenty. I have learned the secret of being content in any and every situation, whether well fed or hungry, whether living in plenty or in want.
PHILIPPIANS 4:12 NIV

What is the secret that Paul understood about contentment, and why would you need it in times of plenty? The shortcoming of both poverty and riches is that we always want more.

The secret to Paul's contentment was that he had experienced God's provision of his spiritual, emotional, and physical needs and knew that he didn't need anything more than trust in the Lord Jesus Christ. You don't need more to make you happy. Jesus is more than enough for you. Once you understand that, you can say, like Paul, that you have learned the secret of being content.

Dear Lord, please forgive me for carrying an attitude of always wanting more. I know that you have given me everything that I need and that you are taking care of me. I pray for contentment in my heart as I trust you in all things.

*R*adiant Reflection

He is the radiance of the glory of God and the exact imprint of his nature,
and he upholds the universe by the word of his power. After making purification for sins,
he sat down at the right hand of the Majesty on high.
HEBREWS 1:3 ESV

Jesus was no ordinary man. We know this of course, but do we acknowledge Jesus as the divine being who had equality with God? When Jesus came to earth, he revealed God's nature to us. Because he is the radiance of God, he reflects a God that is both powerful and loving.

Though Jesus was divine, he came to earth as a man so that he could carry out the will of God. This was to be the ultimate sacrifice for all of humanity, so that our sins would be covered. Jesus, now seated with God in heaven, came for you. He upholds the universe, and he upholds *you* with his Word.

Jesus, I thank you that you humbled yourself as a man so that I might come to know the fullness of God through you. I worship you today because you have revealed yourself as a holy and loving God.

Search Me

Search me, O God, and know my heart; Try me and know my anxious thoughts;
And see if there be any hurtful way in me, And lead me in the everlasting way.
PSALM 139:23-24 NASB

Searching requires looking in every place available to see what is there. Asking God to search your heart means that you are inviting him to know everything that is in it. Vulnerability is hard, particularly when we are battling pride or when we want to hide painful feelings or even sin.

Of course, God already knows your heart, so there is no point in hiding from him. But when you invite him in, you are acknowledging that you might need him to show you things in your heart and mind that need his love and guidance. Know that as you surrender to him, his love will cover all wrong, and he will lead you in the everlasting way.

Search me, O God, and know my heart. Help me to put aside my anxious thoughts and hurtful ways. I want to be led in your everlasting way.

June

Ere the morning lights the skies,
Does there in your heart arise,
Love to Jesus for His tender watchful care?
Do you thank Him for the love
That He sends from Heav'n above,
To protect and lead you thru life's deserts bare?

Do you praise and trust the Lord,
Ev'ry morning, noon, and night?
Do the blessings of His word
Fill your soul with pure delight?

When the noon day sun is bright,
Do your hearts in love unite,
Praising Jesus for His blessings, rich and free?
Do you trust Him ev'ry hour,
For His mercy, grace, and pow'r?
Do you trust His wondrous love eternally?

Do You Praise and Thank Him
By Katharyn Bacon

Delight in His Presence

Then I was constantly at his side.
I was filled with delight day after day,
rejoicing always in his presence.
PROVERBS 8:30 NIV

What does it mean to rejoice in the presence of God? To take delight in simply being with him? The natural outcome of being in God's presence constantly is joy, strength, delight, and a desire to remain there.

The more you soak in his Word and cultivate your relationship with him in your heart, the more he will delight you and satisfy you until you can do nothing but run into his presence daily with intense desire to be with him.

Lord, help me crave your presence. Help me find true delight in being with you.
I pray that nothing in this world would bring me as much joy and satisfaction
as being on my knees before you. I want to delight in your presence day after day.

$\mathscr{I}$nner Beauty

Your beauty should come from within you—the beauty of a gentle and quiet spirit
that will never be destroyed and is very precious to God.
1 PETER 3:4 NCV

God is enraptured by the inner beauty of your true self. It will never matter to him what you look like in the mirror as much as it matters to him what you look like in your soul. Your face, your body, your weight; your human form is not what he fell in love with. The beauty of your spirit is what is precious to God.

God, help me to see myself through your eyes. Help me to spend more time developing my inner beauty than I do touching up my outward beauty. It's so easy for me to get sidetracked by the emphasis on physical appearance in my society, but I want to achieve imperishable beauty by being a woman who has a godly spirit.

Returned Love

I love those who love me,
and those who seek me find me.
PROVERBS 8:17 NIV

With God, we never have to worry about being the one who bestows unrequited love. We always know, with absolute certainty, that our love—no matter how passionate—is even more passionately returned. God loves those who love him; he wants to be sought by you. But even more than that, he longs to be found by you.

Don't think that when you cry out to him you're speaking to thin air. He hears you and loves you. He gives himself to you. Continue in your love for him. Continue in your pursuit of him. He will give himself to you with even greater abandon than you can imagine.

Jesus, thank you for loving me perfectly. Thank you for giving yourself to me fully. Thank you that you have made a way for me to enter your glory and to be loved by you forever.

Continual Praise

From the rising of the sun to its going down
The Lord's name is to be praised.
PSALM 113:3 NKJV

What would it look like to be a woman who praises God from the time she awakens each morning until the time she falls asleep each night? Not only would we be pleasing God as we worship him constantly, but we would also effect an incredible change in our personal outlook.

Intentional, continual praise can only naturally result in intentional, continual joy. When I choose to look at each moment as a moment in which to be thankful and worshipful, then I will find in each moment beauty, joy, and satisfaction.

Lord, I praise you for your love for me. I pray that you would help me to be a woman who praises you all day, every day. I pray that you would cultivate in me an appreciation of your goodness and a longing to worship you constantly.

Powerful Friendship

Flee the evil desires of youth and pursue righteousness, faith, love and peace,
along with those who call on the Lord out of a pure heart.

2 TIMOTHY 2:22 NIV

The Christian life is revolutionary. We are consistently called to step out of the mold and live a life that is different. Being different isn't easy, but when we have other people around us who are living by the same revolutionary standard, we go from being odd to being impassioned.

Such is the power of friendship! In standing side by side, we can encourage one another to grow in our faith, and we can contagiously spread the message of Christ—the message of love and salvation—to the rest of the world.

Lord, bring friends into my life who call on you. Grow my friendships with those who will encourage me to love you more deeply and know you more fully.

Overcome

"I have told you these things, so that in me you may have peace.
In this world you will have trouble. But take heart! I have overcome the world."
JOHN 16:33 NIV

It's so easy to feel overwhelmed by all of the evil in the world. But when we recognize the truth that our God has already conquered all of it, then we can have peace that is beyond anything imaginable. The God who is on our side has—and always will have—the victory over all darkness. We can live our life with the strength and confidence that marks a true conqueror.

Almighty God, I thank you that you have overcome this world. There is nothing so evil that it can overwhelm you, or so fearsome that it can make you back down. I thank you that in you, I have the victory over darkness. I can walk in peace even in the face of adversity because of the greatness of the God I serve.

The Good Father

*"And I will be a father to you,
and you shall be sons and daughters to me,"
says the Lord Almighty.*
2 CORINTHIANS 6:18 ESV

We can easily confuse God's majesty with distance. We begin to think of him as someone who is out of touch with our daily lives—absent and uninterested. But the opposite is true! God is a loving and kind father who takes interest in our deepest thoughts as a father does for his children. He loves us deeply and sensitively, as only a truly good father can. When we adjust our perception of God from far off to profoundly near, our intimacy with him can only deepen.

Thank you, God, that you are a good father. Thank you that you see me as your daughter and that you care deeply about me. Help me to see you as the father that you are, and not as the distant God that the world often portrays you to be.

Right Relationships

Above all, love each other deeply, because love covers over a multitude of sins.
1 PETER 4:8 NIV

Love is always the key ingredient in right relationships because love is synonymous with our creator, God. It was the spilled blood of love that blotted out the sins of man—and only that same love can allow two broken people to support one another in godly relationship.

When we strive to love one another deeply, we not only allow the very essence of Christ to flow through us, we also reveal him to the one we are in relationship with and to the observing world.

God, help me to love deeply those who I am in relationships with. Give me the strength to forgive as you've forgiven me and to cover even a multitude of sins with your love. Bless my friends, my family, and my church through my relationship with them.

Joy That Testifies

*Our mouths were filled with laughter, our tongues with songs of joy.
Then it was said among the nations, "The Lord has done great things for them."*
PSALM 126:2 NIV

True, joyful worship testifies loudly of God's work in our lives. When we speak out in praise, with joy and laughter—because of what God has done for us—the rest of the world will take notice. Often, as Christians, we concentrate completely on walking forward in sober obedience, and we lose sight of the overwhelming joy of the Lord which is our strength.

When we take the time to praise and thank God with happy hearts, even those in the world cannot deny the evidence of God's great work.

Lord, it is a joyful thing to follow you and enjoy your presence. I pray that the joy I feel in your presence would spill out into every facet of my life so that I can be one who proclaims your greatness through my praise.

Relationships of Believers

Rejoice! Strive for full restoration, encourage one another, be of one mind, live in peace. And the God of love and peace will be with you.

2 CORINTHIANS 13:11 NIV

Engaging in healthy, godly relationships between believers is not easy—especially when there is conflict. It can be almost automatic for us to run the other way than to remain and face disagreements or repair a broken relationship.

But when we strive for unity and restoration, for encouragement of one another and for peace, we are literally welcoming the very presence of God into our relationships.

God, I want your presence in my relationships—especially with my fellow believers. I want our love for one another to reflect your love so that the world can see you in us. Give me the strength to fight for resolution, to speak and act with encouragement, and to pursue peace.

Gracious

Yet the Lord longs to be gracious to you; therefore he will rise up to show you compassion. For the Lord is a God of justice. Blessed are all who wait for him!

ISAIAH 30:18 NIV

We can become so overwhelmed by our own shame, troubles, or misconceptions that we miss out on the most simple and beautiful truth—our God greatly desires to show us grace. He doesn't long to show us his anger or his punishment. He doesn't rise up to show us his power and his terrible greatness; he rises up to show us compassion.

When we enter God's presence with this point of view, we are humbled by his love despite his justice—because the punishment we deserve has been outweighed by the grace he longs to give.

I am humbled by the power of your grace for me. Help me to wait for you and to always rely on your grace and your compassion more than my own strength and capacity for goodness.

The Comparison Trap

Let each one examine his own work, and then he will have rejoicing in himself alone, and not in another. For each one shall bear his own load.
GALATIANS 6:4-5 NKJV

Comparison is an easy trap to fall into. When we hear someone else share their story, it can seem as though their life is going smoothly, with everything falling into place exactly as it should. Even when they share great difficulty, we hear their triumphs, making their lives seem far less complicated than our own.

But every single one of us has our dark, confused, and lost moments. And each of those moments will lead us to victory and pride in the work that God has done in us if we let it.

Thank you, Lord, that you are writing my life story, and it doesn't have to look the same as anyone else's. Help me to trust you in the process and not to become distracted by the trap of comparison.

Full Joy

"So you have pain now; but I will see you again, and your hearts will rejoice, and no one will take your joy from you."
JOHN 16:22 NRSV

The joy that comes with the presence of the Lord is a joy that cannot be taken away. When we remember what Christ has done for us, and think about how his grace has changed the eternal course of our lives, we cannot help but be filled with an irrepressible joy.

We may struggle on difficult days, when our lives get hard, to keep sight of the joy of our salvation. But a day is coming when Jesus will return to this earth—setting all things right—and on that day, we will experience our joy in full.

Thank you, Jesus, for the joy of my salvation. Thank you that, in your presence, my joy cannot be taken away from me. I look forward to the day when I will see you face to face, in fullness of joy.

Bold Hope

Since, then, we have such a hope, we act with great boldness.
2 CORINTHIANS 3:12 NRSV

When we fix our eyes on the hope of salvation that we have in Christ Jesus, we cannot help but walk with bravery. When a soldier goes into a battle already knowing that he will come out as the victor, he is able to fight with unprecedented boldness.

As children of God, we are like that soldier. Our battle is already won for us—there is truly nothing to fear. We can walk bravely through life with the hope that makes us bold.

Thank you for the hope I have in you, Lord. Embolden me with confidence so that I can be a testimony of the salvation you've given me. Let me remember your truth constantly so that I will not cease to walk in the boldness of hope.

A God Who Searches

Thus says the Lord GOD: "Indeed I Myself will search for My sheep and seek them out."
EZEKIEL 34:11 NKJV

God values his relationship with you so much that he is willing to go to great lengths to capture your heart. He doesn't just sit stationary, passively waiting for you to approach him. He says that he searches for his sheep—seeking them out.

Have you ever consciously felt God's pursuit of you? Perhaps in Scripture, in a sermon, in a song, or in the words of a friend? He speaks to you because he cares so much about being with you. Allow yourself to be pursued by your God, and respond to his pursuit with a heart that is eager to be loved by him.

Heavenly Father, thank you that you love me enough to pursue me. Thank you for doing what it takes to search for my heart. Let me never grow cold to your pursuit; keep me always ready to respond to your love.

*P*ortion

"The Lord is my portion," says my soul,
"Therefore I have hope in Him."
LAMENTATIONS 3:24 NASB

We live in a world of consumerism where we are continually encouraged to want more. We are taught that with more things will come more joy. But the stuff of this life will never fill the hunger in our souls. The only proper sustenance for a weary soul is a great God.

The Lord is our portion—the perfect portion to fill our emptiness. We need nothing more than him to give us hope, direction, and a future. When we fill ourselves with him, there is nothing more we need.

Help me to remember, God, I don't need to try and fill myself up with the things of this world. All I need to be satisfied by is you. Thank you for giving yourself to me. Thank you for being enough.

Brought Near

In Christ Jesus you who once were far off have been brought near by the blood of Christ.
EPHESIANS 2:13 NKJV

The redemption we have in Jesus has closed the gap that sin once created. We no longer are distant from God; we have been brought near as his children—drawn close in loving relationship.

By living in this truth we are able to cast off shame and formality, having been given the freedom to approach the throne of grace as those who have been redeemed.

I thank you, Jesus, for paying the price for my redemption. Thank you for erasing my debt so that I can stand before God in the closeness of freedom. Help me to stand unashamed in your presence, knowing with certainty that I am clean in your sight.

Understand and Accept

What we have received is not the spirit of the world, but the Spirit who is from God,
so that we may understand what God has freely given us.

1 CORINTHIANS 2:12 NIV

The goodness of God toward us is so far beyond our human capacity for goodness that we struggle to understand it. Our difficulty in understanding God's gifts can ultimately lead to difficulty in our ability to accept them. But at salvation, God puts his spirit within us—enabling us to understand his love, mercy, and grace. With the spirit of God in us, we can both comprehend and accept in full what the Father has given to us.

Heavenly Father, thank you for your great mercy, love, and goodness toward me.
Thank you that through your spirit I can understand and accept all of your good gifts.

Eternal Legacy

The steadfast love of the Lord is from everlasting to everlasting
on those who fear him, and his righteousness to children's children.
PSALM 103:17 NRSV

By putting our faith in Christ, we have entered into an eternal legacy of faith. With our hope and fear placed in God, we receive his steadfast love and his enduring promise. To be the recipient of a love that is everlasting means that you can never fall out of favor with the one who loves you. Steadfast love doesn't change, doesn't run out, and doesn't lose its fervor. Rest in the fact that you are loved forever by the perfect lover.

Thank you, Lord, that you love me with an everlasting love. Thank you for welcoming me into your heavenly family and for establishing me within your lineage. I don't deserve your grace, but you've offered it freely anyway. I know that I am your child and that nothing can change that.

No Reason to Fear

Love the Lord, all you godly ones!
For the Lord protects those who are loyal to him,
but he harshly punishes the arrogant.
So be strong and courageous,
all you who put your hope in the Lord!

PSALM 31:23-24 NLT

Fear should not be a common emotion for a believer. When we live wholeheartedly in the truth that God has already won the victory for us, there is no reason to be afraid. God never leaves us alone and helpless. He is by our side through every situation we face—strengthening us to fight.

We can hold our heads high with courage and confidence in the knowledge that, with God by our side, we have no reason to fear.

Lord, I am often fearful. I worry about the challenges of this world. But I know that you are on my side and that you are stronger than any adversity in life. Thank you that I don't have to live my life in fear because you are with me always—and you make me brave.

Diligent Seekers

The soul of a lazy man desires, and has nothing;
But the soul of the diligent shall be made rich.

PROVERBS 13:4 NKJV

It is a dangerous thing to become comfortable with complacency in our Christian walk. When we are content to stay where we are in our relationship with God, we will not move forward in him. But when we set ourselves to motion in the pursuit of him, then we will be propelled forward in our faith.

If we want to truly know God, then our pursuit of him cannot be passive. We must call ourselves to action, becoming diligent seekers of his presence.

God, don't let me be resigned to apathy in my relationship with you. Keep me continually wanting more of you and longing for your presence. Teach me how to dive deeper in your Word, to discipline myself in prayer, and to persevere in faith.

God's Dwelling Place

Do you not know that you are God's temple and that God's Spirit dwells in you?
1 CORINTHIANS 3:16 ESV

A temple, by definition, is the place where God dwells. In the Old Testament, the people had to travel to the Tabernacle to offer sacrifices and worship God. They relied on a priest to enter the holy place and communicate with God on their behalf.

Under the new covenant, we have the Spirit of the living God dwelling inside our own bodies. At the moment of Christ's death, the curtain separating us from the holy place was ripped in two—symbolizing the end of man's separation from God. Now, his presence is with us always wherever we are, and his glory fills our very being.

Thank you, God, for making a new covenant with us and removing the veil that separated us from your presence. Thank you that I can communicate with you freely and directly. Let me live aware of this glorious privilege I have.

True Love

"All people will know that you are my followers if you love each other."
JOHN 13:35 NCV

We are commanded to love one another. But, love isn't easy. There are parts of every human relationship that are broken. Love is often about repair. You love each other past the difficulty and in spite of the inconvenience. True love is patient enough to rise above challenges and seek solutions. True love doesn't look to satisfy itself; true love gives.

When God defined love, he did it through sacrifice, demonstrating that there is no room for selfishness in love.

God, I want to be known as your follower. Teach me to love like you so I can demonstrate your love to those around me. Give me the strength required to be selfless in my love and devoted in my relationships.

Commissioned to Boldness

"As Moses lifted up the serpent in the wilderness, even so must the Son of Man be lifted up; so that whoever believes will in Him have eternal life."

JOHN 3:14-15 NASB

Moses complied even with God's most awkward, uncomfortable commands. Once, he obediently constructed a brass snake, placed it on a pole, and ordered everyone to stare at it if bitten by deadly snakes. The Israelites must have scratched their heads, but the ones who actually trusted and looked to the snake were healed. This story foreshadows the sacrifice of Jesus on the cross: death came through the first Adam, yet salvation comes through the last Adam as we look to him in faith.

We have a commission similar to Moses': we *lift Jesus high*, telling people to look to him for eternal life. It may seem awkward, but we also set aside our self-awareness. We set before us Jesus Christ and his love for the people he came to save.

Jesus, you have people out there who need you, and I'm the "you" they see. You were never a bystander, so please make me bold, casting all those concerns and weights over my shoulder as I move forward in faith. Faith pleases you, so please grant me faith: make me bold in action.

JUNE 25

Jesus Keeps You in the Race

"Do not be afraid; you have done all this evil. Yet do not turn aside from following the Lord, but serve the Lord with all your heart."

1 SAMUEL 12:20 ESV

We often struggle, thinking we need to forgive ourselves because we lack peace about the sins of our past. The fact of the matter is this: Jesus' forgiveness is what is important, and if Jesus sets you free, you have no opinion in the matter any longer. Jesus forgave your sins. He brushes the dirt off your knees, kissing and bandaging your wounds. Now you can run again.

In running, never stop for the sake of hopelessness or doubt. Never take your hand off the plow because you feel unworthy. You never earned the right to serve God. Jesus is the one who bought you, and he is the one who forgave you. If the one who will judge all things has declared you clean, then you are a bride who is spotless.

God, help me to serve you with all my heart. Free me from condemnation and grief. Help me to truly know your love and forgiveness. Thank you for redeeming me and drawing me to you.

187

Remember God's Faithfulness

Those who love me, I will deliver; I will protect those who know my name.
When they call to me, I will answer them; I will be with them in trouble,
I will rescue them and honor them.
PSALM 91:14-15 NRSV

When we read God's Word, we glue our need to God's provision. We read the words on the page and realize God has helped people with the same needs as ours. Whether it's for love or wisdom, provision or righteousness, Jesus has all we need. He is a generous giver, and he has beckoned us closer to receive what he has for us—including intimacy with him.

Read through his Word and be trained of him. Let the Holy Spirit teach you all things as you ponder and reflect. Read the Psalms for comfort and encouragement; study the Proverbs for deeper wisdom. God's Word is written for you, and it belongs to you.

Lord, please help me read your Word and understand it the way you intend. I trust you to grow my faith and meet my needs as I learn and profit from your wisdom. I love you!

Strength Every Morning

Lord, be gracious to us; we long for you.
Be our strength every morning, our salvation in time of distress.
ISAIAH 33:2 NIV

In times of crisis, each new morning demands our strength. In seasons of difficulty, waking brings with it worry, fear, and distress. We all look for strength in different places; some of us find security in financial wellness, others in physical health, still others in community and friendships. But if Christ is the ultimate source of strength, then each new morning we will open his Word and find truth to counteract worry with peace, fear with understanding, and distress with steadfastness. His grace will make us more than able to rise each morning with strength for the day.

I need your strength, Lord, to face the hardships in my life. Each new morning I want to run to your presence so that I can be filled by your spirit and made ready in your love.

Unless the Lord

Unless the Lord builds a house, the work of the builders is wasted.
Unless the Lord protects a city, guarding it with sentries will do no good.
PSALM 127:1 NLT

To attempt any great work apart from Christ is meaningless. Without seeking to work alongside him in his will, our efforts are wasted and our goals are futile. But when we choose to partner with Almighty God in the work he is already accomplishing, then we experience the joy of his blessing and the reward of his presence.

Wait for God. Ask him to reveal to you where he is working and how he would like you to join him. Ask him to call on you as he did the disciples—by telling you to follow him and then by leading you directly into his will.

Guide me, Lord, into being an effective participant in your will. Don't let me build my own kingdoms apart from your purposes. Help me to obey you in all things so that I might accomplish your will.

The Goodness in Waiting

The Lord is wonderfully good to those who wait for him, to those who seek for him.
It is good both to hope and wait quietly for the salvation of the Lord.
LAMENTATIONS 3:25-26 TLB

Have you ever watched other people enjoy their "happily-ever-afters" while you sat wondering if yours would ever come? Sometimes it feels as though everyone else has their lives perfectly in order while your own is in some type of chaos. Finding yourself waiting is challenging enough without watching everyone else rush ahead of you. But God promises goodness to those who are kept waiting. If you choose to seek the Lord as you wait, he will reveal himself to you in a sweeter way than you could have known otherwise.

Help me, God, to see waiting as a blessed opportunity to know your goodness.
Teach me to wait quietly and with hope for you.

Grit of Grace

Don't listen to everything people say, or you might hear your servant insulting you. You know that many times you have insulted others.
ECCLESIASTES 7:21-22 NCV

There is something so awful about hearing that someone has spoken badly about you behind your back. You want a chance to defend yourself against such an unfair attack. But instead of quickly becoming angry, consider whether or not you have spoken similar negative words about someone else in the heat of a moment. When we recognize our own failings, we free ourselves up to forgive even the most insensitive of offenders. It is in these moments that we come face to face with the grit of grace—understanding the depth of its reach and the extent of its value.

Lord, it's not easy to be wronged by others, but I ask that you would give me the strength to forgive, just as I so desperately need forgiveness.

July

From ev'ry stormy wind that blows,
From ev'ry swelling tide of woes,
There is a calm, a sure retreat;
'Tis found beneath the mercy seat.

There is a place where Jesus sheds
The oil of gladness on our heads,
A place than all besides more sweet;
It is the blood bo't mercy seat.

There, there on eagle's wings we soar,
And sin and sense seem all no more,
And heav'n comes down our souls to greet,
And glory crowns the mercy seat.

From Every Stormy Wind
By Hugh Stowell

Simply Listen

After the earthquake, there was a fire, but the Lord was not in the fire.
After the fire, there was a quiet, gentle sound.

1 KINGS 19:12 NCV

Hurricanes, tornadoes, tsunamis, and the like are sometimes referred to as acts of God. This means the occurrences were outside of human control, but the expression can lead us to misunderstand God and how he works.

Elijah knew exactly where to find God. After being told to wait in a cave for the presence of the Lord, he waited through a great wind, an earthquake, and a raging fire. Only after, when he heard a quiet, gentle sound, did he sense God's presence and go out to meet him.

Father, I long to hear your whisper. I yearn to experience your presence. Help me to see past the fires that command my attention, to look beyond the earthquakes, and simply listen.

Generous Heart

A generous person will prosper;
whoever refreshes others will be refreshed.
PROVERBS 11:25 NIV

On the surface, this verse may seem to suggest that we give in order to get. Looking deeper, we see beyond. Think of a child reluctantly breaking a cookie into pieces, sizing them up, and handing over the smaller one with a scowl. The giver was most certainly not refreshed by this exchange.

Giving is an act; generosity is a condition of the heart. Only a generous heart is refreshed by giving. It is this generous heart our Father waits eagerly to bless.

Lord, you are the generous one. You watch and you wait, graciously showering your blessings on those who share from their hearts. Refresh my spirit to see the beauty in pouring into others. Give me a heart that longs to give. Give me a heart like yours.

A Sure Foundation

In that day he will be your sure foundation,
providing a rich store of salvation, wisdom, and knowledge.
The fear of the Lord will be your treasure.
ISAIAH 33:6 NLT

Think back to a time you were filled with fear. What caused you to feel unsafe? Whether from physical danger or emotional insecurity, you need never allow fear to take hold of you again.

Fear of the Lord, reverence for all he is and all he's done, replaces all fear. Once you have been saved by God's grace, once you know him and understand the foundation on which you stand, no power on earth can shake you. You are safe; you are his.

Father, I stand on your truth; the ground beneath me cannot be moved. The more I know you, the more I understand this. Your gift of salvation means as long as I am yours, I am safe. Thank you, Lord.

Truly Free

*Out of my distress I called on the Lord;
the Lord answered me and set me free.*
PSALM 118:5 ESV

Today, all across America, people celebrate freedom. At first glance, these gatherings may seem simply to relish the freedom to light fireworks, enjoy triple-berry pie, and inhale Aunt Mary's potato salad, but beneath the surface lies an opportunity for true worship.

As you wipe that tear from your eye during the National Anthem, consider what your freedom really means—not just as an American, but as an adopted daughter of the Almighty.

Father, just calling you by that name gives me more freedom than some will ever know. How can I thank you for setting me free from fear, from sin, and even from death? Because you choose to call me yours, I am truly free. Help me to live and share this incredible truth.

For His Glory

I will do whatever you ask in my name, so that the Father may be glorified in the Son.
JOHN 14:13 NIV

You have the power of Christ at your lips. How does this resonate with you? And how do you reconcile this incredible truth with seemingly unanswered prayers?

He promises to do whatever we ask in his name—in order to glorify the Father. Jesus sees well past today. Perhaps to truly bring glory to God we sometimes need an answer other than "yes," no matter how sincere our hearts and how worthy our requests.

Jesus, I trust you. I know a "no" from you is really a "yes" for me. Help me see past my immediate concerns to the grand, perfect plan of the Father. Align my heart with yours, so all I would ask in your name would bring glory to God.

No Plan B

My victory and honor come from God alone.
He is my refuge, a rock where no enemy can reach me.
PSALM 62:7 NLT

When applying to colleges, students are invariably advised to have, in addition to their first choice—the place they really want to end up—a fallback school, a Plan B. It's less than ideal, but virtually guaranteed to work.

In matters of faith, God is the single source of our safety, our only means to victory. The good news: if we are truly his, we don't need a Plan B.

Lord, you are my first choice. Your love, plan, and provision are all I need. I know this, yet I still worry and have to resist the desire to try to control things myself. Help me rest in the safety of your arms and claim the honor and victory I have in you.

In the Light

With You is the fountain of life;
In Your light we see light.
PSALM 36:9 NKJV

How would you explain color to a blind person? What is blue, and what makes it unique from red, purple, or green? In order to understand pink, you need to have experienced it.

It is the same with goodness, love, and light. In order to recognize it, we must know it. In order to know it, we must know the Father. He is the one true source of all light, of all that is good.

Abba, I want to live in the light! You are the source of its warmth; its life-giving power is from you. As the source of all that is good, you are all I need. Thank you, Lord, for your ever-flowing fountain. I drink in your goodness today, seeing evidence of your light all around me.

Peace Is Mine

May the Lord of peace himself give you peace at all times in every way.

2 THESSALONIANS 3:16 ESV

Think of a time when your life was absolutely perfect. How long did it last? Whether a moment, an hour, or even several days, eventually the shine wore off and real life crept back in. Here on earth, things will never be perfect.

This is why the peace of the Lord is such a valuable treasure! Jesus has overcome the world, so when we give him our hearts, his peace forms a barrier between us and everything that would steal our joy.

Lord, when the world is getting to me, when troubles and pressures seem to swallow me, let this be a sign to me; I have wandered from you. In you, only in you, peace is mine.

Best Day Ever

A single day in your courts
is better than a thousand anywhere else!
I would rather be a gatekeeper in the house of my God
than live the good life in the homes of the wicked.

PSALM 84:10 NLT

Remember the best day of your life. Would you trade nearly three years of your life for that precious memory, let's say living to 85 instead of 88? Now magnify the greatness of that wonderful day beyond your imagining; picture a day in God's presence. How many ordinary days would that be worth?

Answer this next question thoughtfully: would you rather be poor, yet surrounded by people full of love and integrity, or wealthy among those who compromise morality and goodness as a matter of course?

Lord, examine my heart. Am I living a life that reflects my desire for you? What would you have me change? Where would you have me go?

The Privilege of Suffering

He has graciously granted you the privilege not only of believing in Christ,
but of suffering for him as well.
PHILIPPIANS 1:29 NRSV

By its very definition, suffering is not enjoyable. Yet we are told that as believers we are granted the privilege of suffering for Christ. Suffering as a blessing? Something to be desired?

Consider what Christ suffered for us. Hard to imagine, isn't it? But if we willingly place ourselves in diffcult or painful situations in his name, we draw a little closer. To experience pain while pursuing him is to know more of his heart—a great privilege indeed.

Lord, I will gladly suer to know you more. Facing ridicule for holding onto my morals in a fallen world, feeling the pain of blisters and sore muscles as I work alongside fellow believers in a hurting nation, I feel you. Grant me the privilege, Jesus.

Perfect Peace

You will keep in perfect peace all who trust in you,
all whose thoughts are fixed on you!
ISAIAH 26:3 NLT

What robs you of your peace? Thoughts of unpaid bills, unfavorable diagnoses, and unfulfilled dreams creep in unexpectedly, threatening the security we feel in our Lord's protection. But they don't have to.

These words in Isaiah are not a bargain: if we do this, he grants that. They are an observation. When we trust God fully, and keep our minds on him, we naturally feel peace. Because he is perfect, only perfect peace can come from trusting him. Thoughts fixed on him are thoughts steeped in tranquility.

Father, you bring peace not as a reward, but as an inevitable outcome. When I trust you, what can I possibly fear? When I think of you, what can disturb the beauty of those thoughts? In you, peace is my promise.

An Arm to Lean On

The everlasting God is your place of safety,
and his arms will hold you up forever.
DEUTERONOMY 33:27 NCV

In comedy, it's not uncommon to see a character lean against an unstable surface only to fall as they realize they misplaced their trust. What looked like a wall was actually a revolving door. Arms flail, legs fly, we laugh.

It's a little less funny when we're the ones flailing. God wants only stable surfaces for us to lean against, which is why we are called to trust him with all our hearts. Popularity, financial success, knowledge, and even relationships are ultimately just revolving doors.

Lord, you are my foundation. Please help me to trust your timing, your plan, and your provision over anything I think I know. Yours is the arm I want to lean on when I am hurting; only you will keep me upright and secure.

*L*ike a Child

"Truly I tell you, anyone who will not receive the kingdom of God like a little child will never enter it."

MARK 10:15 NIV

Take a break from the mid-July heat and picture Christmas morning: children running down the stairs, tearing gleefully into packages. Every gift brings fresh exclamations of gratitude and joy. Each shiny ornament holds wonder.

This, we are told, is the only way to receive the kingdom of God. Like a child on Christmas morning, we must open up to wonder, enthusiasm, and thanks. How is this working in your life? Do you need his help in order to freely receive his gifts?

Father, I welcome your kingdom with the gratitude and joy of a child.
Eagerly, I accept the gifts you have for me. I wonder at your beauty and perfection.
Gratefully and unreservedly, I receive your love and blessings.

By His Wounds

He was pierced for our transgressions, he was crushed for our iniquities;
the punishment that brought us peace was on him,
and by his wounds we are healed.

ISAIAH 53:5 NIV

"I can't believe you did that for me!" Seldom do we feel more loved than when someone has gone through something—suffered—for us. How much, then, must Jesus love us?

No amount of suffering could truly be a fair exchange for all the world's sin, yet his pain was essential. Why? So we would feel the weight of it. The weight of our sin, and the weight of his great, great love.

Lord, it breaks my heart to imagine you in agony. To know you did it for me brings me to my knees. I can never deserve what you did for me; I can only accept the healing you bring with your precious, perfect love.

JULY 15

Renewal

You were dead because of your sins and because your sinful nature was not yet cut away. Then God made you alive with Christ, for he forgave all our sins.

COLOSSIANS 2:13 NLT

As new Christians, we may naively think the transformation is permanent. We're his, therefore we're changed. While true, it's not the end of the story.

As long as we are here, we'll face temptation from the world. Renewal is an ongoing process. Each time we find ourselves conforming, we must re-transform, renew. What a blessing it is to know that we can. Again and again, he welcomes us.

Father, your will is good, pleasing, and perfect. Mine is not. Sometimes I want what the world offes. Thank you for endless trips to the well of your forgiveness. Over and over, you transform my heart and renew my mind, making me yours.

Openly and Utterly

"Let the little children come to me, and do not hinder them,
for the kingdom of God belongs to such as these."
MARK 10:14 NIV

Jesus loved children. The Bible doesn't have many stories of him with children, but those we do have make it clear: he found them to be incredibly special.

What was it? Children have a way of just...being, without any contrivance. Perhaps it was this authenticity. Maybe their absolute dependence was what captivated his heart.

Lord, I approach you today as a child: trusting, unreserved, and wholly dependent on you. If I hurt, I'll cry. If I'm joyful, I'll dance. I recognize my great need for you. I love you openly and utterly. Help me to desire nothing more than to rest in your arms and know your love.

Start Here

The beginning of wisdom is this: Get wisdom.
Though it cost all you have, get understanding.
PROVERBS 4:7 NIV

If only all instructions were so straightforward: the first step on the path to wisdom? Realize how vital wisdom is. Understanding is worth everything we have. According to this verse, nothing matters more.

Let's take a moment to let this soak in. Without true understanding, everything we gain may be the wrong thing. No matter how successful or happy, or even how much good we do in the world, if we don't "get it," we may miss out on his plan—and nothing could possibly be worth that.

Father, grant me eyes that see, ears that hear, and a heart that looks and listens! Help me to gain wisdom, so I may live in your will. Nothing I accomplish, nothing I gain, means anything if it is not part of your perfect plan.

Astounding Love

"No, for I will give a sevenfold punishment to anyone who kills you."
Then the Lord put a mark on Cain to warn anyone who might try to kill him.
GENESIS 4:15 NLT

This is God speaking to Cain. Yes, Cain. The murderer. He's just exiled him for his crime, but he's also just given him protection.

God's love for us and his capacity to forgive us knows no boundaries. Anyone killing Cain could expect a punishment seven times more severe than the one Cain himself received for killing his own brother. That is love. And this is the God we serve!

Lord, your love astounds me. If you would provide this protection to Cain,
an unrepentant murderer, to what lengths would you go to protect me? I can't fathom it.
Nor can I ever deserve it. I can only thank you, again and again.

_____

_____

_____

_____

_____

_____

_____

_____

_____

Joyful in Tribulation

I am filled with comfort. I am exceedingly joyful in all our tribulation.
2 CORINTHIANS 7:4 NKJV

Imagine being in prison. Now picture yourself joyful in prison. What would it take? Can you honestly imagine it? On our own, it would be impossible. The circumstances simply wouldn't allow it. But we are not alone.

The apostle Paul exemplifies many Christian attributes, but perhaps none more poignantly than joy. Joy is happiness regardless of circumstances— untouchable peace. It was Paul's, and it can be ours.

Holy Spirit, come fill me with your joy. Apart from you, comfort evades me as the troubles of this world surround me. I long for a peace that defies my circumstances, that passes all understanding. I surrender my feeble human attempts at happiness, and invite you to replace them with joy.

Seek His Face

Seek the Lord and His strength;
Seek His face continually.

PSALM 105:4 NASB

Meeting someone in a crowd, we scan each face in search of their familiar features. Once we've found them, we feel relief, happiness, a sense of home.

This is the way our Lord wants to be sought. He desires not just presence or conversation with us, but intimacy. "Seek my face," he says. Not just forgiveness, not just answered prayer, but real, face-to-face connection.

Lord, I spend most of my time looking for things. From the lofty (meaning, purpose, security) to the mundane (bargains, missing earrings, mislaid phones), I am always seeking. Help me remember, Holy Spirit, that nothing matters more than to seek the face of God. In your presence, all is well; all is beautiful. I long for intimacy with you.

Totally Committed

The Lord is faithful; he will strengthen you and guard you from the evil one.
2 THESSALONIANS 3:3 NLT

Faithful friends never betray you.
A faithful dog sticks close to your side.
A faithful spouse has eyes only for you.

The Lord is faithful. Allow this incredible truth to strengthen and sustain you as you face whatever the enemy has planned today. God will never betray you; the creator of the universe never leaves your side; Jesus will never choose another over you.

Lord, who am I that you are unwavering in your commitment to me? My own faithfulness wavers from day to day. I see things I want; I face issues I'd rather not, and sin lures me away from you. Today, God, I am totally committed to you. I marvel anew at your love and draw my strength from the wellspring of your faithfulness.

Under His Arm

Let all who take refuge in you be glad;
let them ever sing for joy.
Spread your protection over them,
that those who love your name may rejoice in you.

PSALM 5:11 NIV

Summer heat sometimes brings summer storms. With a tornado heading your way, you'd seek protection. You'd get low, beneath something sturdy and strong.

The Lord wants to be your shelter from the storms of life. He asks us to humble ourselves—to get low—before him and take refuge under his strong arms. The reward: not just protection, but songs of joy!

Father, when I am smart enough to come to you for protection, you form an impenetrable shield between me and anything life can dish out. No circumstance can rob me of the joy of being under your shelter. I rejoice in this truth, and sing today of your awesome power

Abiding Love

Satisfy us in the morning with your unfailing love,
that we may sing for joy and be glad all our days.
PSALM 90:14 NIV

Think of brand-new love, where the newness and the enthusiasm are almost overwhelming. Whether a romance, a new pet, or even a new fitness plan, that feeling may or may not take root.

Let us make sure we are rooted in our relationship with Jesus. Has the joy of discovering him given way to the deeper joy of knowing him and walking with him each day?

Lord, my heart overflows with thankfulness as I consider all you've done for me.
Strengthen my faith, Jesus, as I live my life in your deep, abiding strength and love.
I sink my roots down right here, into my love for you.

Naked and Exposed

Nothing in all creation is hidden from God. Everything is naked and exposed before his eyes, and he is the one to whom we are accountable.
HEBREWS 4:13 NLT

Going through old family photos, we inevitably come across the "naked and proud" photos. Babies and toddlers entirely exposed, and entirely pleased with themselves. Adorable photos. We are utterly charmed.

Most of us have known a child like that. Some of us *were* a child like that. Ponder this wonderful truth: you are still that child to God. There is absolutely nothing about you he doesn't see and doesn't know, and he finds you every bit as precious as a baby in a bathtub.

God, I can barely comprehend your love. You see everything, and still you adore me. How can this be? I lay my life before you, and I thank you for your grace.

Friendship

Do not forsake your friend or a friend of your family,
and do not go to your relative's house when disaster strikes you—
better a neighbor nearby than a relative far away.

PROVERBS 27:10 NIV

Much is made of the importance of family, but the Bible makes it clear we are also meant to share our lives with friends. These are the people that are with you simply because you are you. What a precious and wonderful gift!

Loving, committed friendship with people in our communities is God's plan—and his gift—for us. Take care to nurture those relationships, and to be the kind of friend others seek out in a time of need.

Father, today I thank you for friendship. As I spend some time thinking of the people you place in my life, help me to see the unique and wonderful way you've made each of them, and show me how to love them better.

This Heart-Longing

My heart said of you, "Go, worship him."
So I come to worship you, Lord.
PSALM 27:8 NCV

When struggling with an important decision, we're often advised to listen to our hearts. The wisdom is that we already know what to do; when we tune into our longing, the answer is waiting.

With the Holy Spirit an active part of your life, your heart will often be directed toward the Lord. In times of need, in times of joy, listen to your heart and worship your God.

Father God, when I search my heart, I find you. My heart longs for you. Because I will never be home until I am in heaven worshipping you for all eternity, this heart-longing is always with me. No song or prayer expresses all you are and all you've done for me. Today and every day, I worship and celebrate you.

Home

"I will come back and take you to be with me that you also may be where I am."
JOHN 14:3 NIV

Where is home? For some, the place we came from will always be home. Others of us have found or created it in a new place, one of our own choosing. Maybe home isn't even a place for you, but a feeling you get with certain people.

Regardless of where we feel at home here on earth, the Lord wants us to remember our true home, which is in heaven with him. Those fleeting feelings of security and perfection are fleeting for just this reason. You are a citizen of heaven.

Lord, thank you for reminding me where I belong. Thank you for your perfect sacrifice so I can claim my citizenship in your holy kingdom. You are my home.

Lost and Found

I have gone astray like a lost sheep; seek Your servant,
For I do not forget Your commandments.
PSALM 119:176 NASB

The advent of GPS and smart phones has made it more rare, but still, occasionally, we may find ourselves lost. With no familiar landmarks and no one to follow, our only option is to ask for help.

We can lose sight of the route on our faith walk as well and find ourselves in that same predicament: lost. For spiritual disorientation, the same remedy exists: call for help.

Lord, you are my spiritual GPS. Any time I find myself wandering from the path you have set for me, the voice of your Spirit gently leads me back. I remember your command—to love God with all I am—and the route I am on begins to look familiar again. As I share your love with others, I am found.

He Is Watching

The Lord will watch over your coming and going
both now and forevermore.
PSALM 121:8 NIV

If you've ever been to a park with a small child, you know this one thing: don't take your eyes off them. Both danger and delight lurk on every swing, every slide. Other children may be new friends, or may throw sand in your little charge's face. You have to be there, watching.

To God, you are that child. Your Abba never takes his eyes off you. He wants you to experience swinging high, making friends, and climbing ladders. You'll get a few scrapes and bruises, but because he is with you, you'll be okay.

Abba, the more I know you, the more I understand how you love. You don't keep me from getting hurt; that's part of living, which is why I'm here. Your love watches, assures: I'll be okay.

s I Should Be

There is surely a future hope for you,
and your hope will not be cut off.
PROVERBS 23:18 NIV

God made you. Carefully, intentionally, he made you. And he knew exactly what he was doing, and why. Even the desires of your heart are there on purpose: to lead the Father's plan for your life.

The next time you doubt your worth, remember these words. The next time your question your purpose, look to your passions. What wonderful things did he prepare in advance for you to do?

Lord, sometimes I doubt myself. All I see are my many flaws, and all I feel is the weight of my sin. Thank you for reminding me that to you, I am exactly as I should be. I am who and how you made me. Lead me, Father, to the good you'd have me do.

All for Good

"You intended to harm me, *Joseph* but God intended it all for good.
He brought me to this position so I could save the lives of many people."
GENESIS 50:20 NLT

We don't like thinking about this, but sometimes we have to go through horrible things to become the person God wants us to be. We can't always see past "now," especially when it's hard, to realize that rather than *happening* to us, our circumstances are *leading* us to where we need to be.

Even in the wake of unspeakable tragedy, the Lord leads us through, holds us close, and shapes us into who we're meant to be. Within God's perfect plan, even other people's sins against us can be used for good.

Lord, you make all things beautiful. You take grief, loss, betrayal, and shame and turn them into rejoicing, renewal, and grace. With you, it is all for good.

August

Dread not the things that are ahead,
The burdens great, the sinking sands,
The thorns that o'er the path are spread,
God holds the future in His hands.

God holds the future in His hands,
And every heart He understands;
On Him depend; He is your Friend;
He holds the future in His hands.

Live close to Him and trust His love,
Assured that while on earth we roam,
Whate'er may come, He bends above
To guide His children safely home.

God Holds the Future in His Hands
By James Rowe

Look to the Mountains

I lift up my eyes to the mountains—where does my help come from?
My help comes from the Lord, the Maker of heaven and earth.
PSALM 121:1-2 NIV

It would seem that the psalmist is tapping into a tendency that we have—to look somewhere other than God for help. We might even be looking at grand, promising entities like a mountain. When someone is desperate for strength, their eyes can frantically search around for something, anything, to offer them help.

Have you looked to the mountain? Did it offer you anything? Did it save you or strengthen you? The psalmist immediately answers that question: help comes from the Lord. And then he goes on to unpack why the Lord is more supreme than a mountain—he's the *maker* of the mountain. And he's the maker of heaven and earth. Don't look to the created; look to the creator for help. You will not be left in want.

Father, thank you that mountains are but a weak reflection of your strength, stability, and power. Help me look squarely on you for my help.

Seek and Find

"Keep on asking, and you will receive what you ask for. Keep on seeking, and you will find. Keep on knocking, and the door will be opened to you."

LUKE 11:9 NLT

Have you ever sought after something with no guarantee of a return? Maybe you participated in an Easter egg hunt as a child and went away empty handed, or took an ocean tour boat with the hope of seeing whales but returned to the dock with only the sight of sea waves banging against your ship. We are prone to seek after many prizes, but few treasure hunts will guarantee any return on your dollar or your time.

There is one treasure hunt you can guarantee will leave you fulfilled. Seek God and you will find him. He promises this in his Word. You can know with certainty that *any* investment you make in seeking him will be rewarded.

Jesus, help me boldly approach you so I can find help in my hour of need. Thank you that I can confidently seek you and know that in my seeking, I will never leave empty handed.

*B*ecoming a Caster

Cast all your anxiety on him because he cares for you.
1 PETER 5:7 NIV

We are boldly called to do something that is entirely unnatural. Cast our anxieties on the Lord? What a word! Have you ever been anxious? Have you ever been paralyzed with fear? What should we do as God's children? His advice is simple. Cast it to him.

Casting means to throw out aggressively. Sometimes we habitually turn into anxious people, facing every trial with fear and not our promised peace. In training yourself to be a "caster" of anxiety and not a holder of it, you will enjoy abundant freedom that you had previously only wished for.

Father, give me the grace to break the habit of anxiety
and help me learn to enjoy the freedom you died for me to have.

Delivered from Fear

I sought the Lord, and he answered me
and delivered me from all my fears.
PSALM 34:4 ESV

For various reasons, many of us grow up with certain fears in our hearts. Often the fear is unwarranted, but sometimes it's based on tragic circumstances. When fear's seeds sink into our hearts, they can grow giant trees of debilitating behaviors that paralyze us from functioning normally.

Praise the Lord that we have an advocate who has the power to demolish every stronghold and fear that has ever gripped us. The simple formula to access the power of our deliverer is to seek him. God's job is to deliver; our role is to seek. Seeking takes perseverance and endurance, but as we do, we can rest in the promise of his Word that he will indeed deliver us from all our fears.

Jesus, thank you that you hold the power to deliver me from my fears.
Please give me the endurance to persevere in seeking and trusting you for my healing.

*B*uried Talents

"Whoever has will be given more, and they will have an abundance.
Whoever does not have, even what they have will be taken from them."
MATHEW 25:29 NIV

God, in his well-executed plan, endowed his children with talents. In Matthew 25:15, we get a small glimpse of his purpose in putting unique gifts within each of us. God alone decides how many talents he will entrust us with. These talents are graciously endowed to us and are not actually meant for our own benefit; they are intended to be a blessing to others.

Is the thought of exercising your talents so overwhelming in your already hectic schedule that you have chosen to bury them instead? Buried talents do nobody any good. Exercising those talents will actually become life giving to you.

Jesus, please push me forward, even when I push back.
I pray for the grace to serve in the way that you equipped and created me to.

Thorns

In order to keep me from becoming conceited, I was given a thorn in my flesh...
Three times I pleaded with the Lord to take it away from me.
2 CORINTHIANS 12:7-8 NIV

Would you like some great news today? Every child of God is profoundly imperfect. In addition to being imperfect, we all have besetting weaknesses. Many of these weaknesses can be managed and some, through the power of God, can actually be healed. But rest assured, weaknesses will not altogether go away. Once one is conquered, you will often find that another gets exposed. They are part of humanity.

What is your thorn? What area do you wrestle in continually? Paul, the great hero of our faith, also wrestled with a besetting weakness. God wants us to remain weak so that we can be strong in him. We are forced to remain in the place of humility, clinging to God for strength and comfort.

Thank you, God, for giving me thorns. Even though I don't like them, I know they are good for me. They keep me humble and trusting in you. Help me to cling to you for strength in every area of my life.

True Strength

I pray that from his glorious, unlimited resources he will empower you with inner strength through his Spirit. Then Christ will make his home in your hearts as you trust in him. Your roots will grow down into God's love and keep you strong.

EPHESIANS 3:16-17 NLT

Do you know today that God has not asked you to be strong? You won't hear that from TV, magazines, or social media. God didn't make you to be a model of *your strength* for others. He did make you to be a model of *his strength* though.

There is a big difference between being strong in our own power and being strong in God's power. The key to strength in God starts with acknowledging our profound weaknesses. When we own our weakness, it is an act of humility. God never asks us to be strong; he wants us to be dependent on him. Someone who is humble and dependent gets the gift of God's supernatural strength.

Jesus, grant me, by your grace, the revelation of your strength in my weakness.

232

Pouring

In the last days I will pour out my Spirit on all kinds of people.
ACTS 2:17 NCV

Sometimes visual aids help us understand a concept that would otherwise be lost. Did you pour anything this morning? Milk on cereal, water on plants, creamer in coffee, or bathwater on a child's head? Pouring is very different than dripping. It's more than a small steady stream of liquid. Pouring indicates something gushing from a source. It is an unleashing that saturates.

God uses the same terminology of what he does when he gives his Spirit. He says he pours it out. God knows that you don't just need a trickle or a sprinkling of his Spirit. He delights in pouring more of himself over you as you ask and wait. It is his delight and his gift to you—and it will never run out.

Father, thank you that you aren't reserved or selfish with your Spirit. You are extravagant and abundant in your pouring. I ask you again today, please pour out your Spirit on me.

Hearing Truth

"When he, the Spirit of truth, comes, he will guide you into all truth."
JOHN 16:13 NIV

Do you have a steady diet of truth-hearing in your life? Whether we like it or not, every one of us in varying degrees is constantly hearing ungodly wisdom. The world will not counsel you in the ways of God. It will urge you to hate your body, hold a grudge, and accept every sin under the sun. These messages will be spoken loudly.

It is of utmost importance to regularly hear, read, and meditate on truth. It won't always be natural to remember or believe, so it is critical that we daily refresh our mind and our spirit with it.

Father, please reveal to me areas where I think like the world and not like you. I ask that you, by your Spirit, will renew my mind and make me like you.

An Anchored Soul

Then you will experience God's peace, which exceeds anything we can understand.
His peace will guard your hearts and minds as you live in Christ Jesus.
PHILIPPIANS 4:7 NLT

No matter how uncertain your future may be, or how confusing your circumstances, your life is firmly established on the faithfulness of God. Nothing can shake you when your eternity is secured.

The peace that is available to the heart of a believer is beyond our human understanding. When we have the peace of Christ, we cannot be shaken to our core. We may feel overwhelmed, and we may even begin to lose our faith, but deep within us our souls are anchored and cannot be moved.

Thank you, Lord, for your peace. I know that no matter what I face I have the privilege of a hope secured in you. Help me to run to you in times of trouble, seeking your peace above any other comfort.

Finishing Touches

Looking unto Jesus, the author and finisher of our faith.
HEBREWS 12:2 NKJV

Have you ever watched an artist paint a picture? The artist begins with an unblemished white canvas waiting to be transformed into a piece of art. As you watch, at different times it seems as if the painting could be finished. But in the last few moments, the artist applies the fine detail and extra colors that make the painting truly complete.

God is also a finisher. Our faith begins with God as the author. As we walk with him, we find ourselves believing that once he gets the ball rolling, it's up to us to finish the task. Praise the Lord that he declares it is his responsibility to not only author our faith but also to finish it. Don't walk away before he is finished! Those final touches can make a precious masterpiece.

Thank you, Father, that you will complete that which you began in my life.
I trust you to be the finisher of my faith.

Just Run

Let us also lay aside every weight and the sin that clings so closely.
HEBREWS 12:1 NRSV

Have you ever observed the clinging power of a used dryer sheet? When a load of laundry is complete, the used dryer sheet is often stuck to a piece of clothing so tightly that it looks like it has been sewn on top of it. However, simply pulling on a corner of that clinging dryer sheet will remove it.

The nature of sin is to cling to us and grip us. Like a dryer sheet, sin won't simply fall off us. It takes an intentional action to remove or resist it. But it *can* be conquered. If you are casually swiping away the sin in your life, perhaps it's time for a different approach. Maybe it's time to run from the sin and into God's presence.

Jesus, I ask for your Spirit to encourage me that I don't need to be a slave to the clinging sin. I can instead run to you and you will remove it from me.

Divine Citizenship

He has granted to us his precious and very great promises, so that through them you may become partakers of the divine nature, having escaped from the corruption that is in the world.
2 PETER 1:3-4 ESV

Do you remember where you were on September 11, 2001? Not since December 7, 1941, at Pearl Harbor, had we seen an attack on American soil. Sure, we had fought in wars since that date, but the wars were always in another country. September 11 showed us that we weren't invincible to an enemy attack—and our epicenter of commerce and trade could be deeply shaken.

This is one of the reasons it is important to rejoice that while many of us might be Americans, it is not our only citizenship. If we have given our lives to God, we have become citizens of his kingdom. We do not know what will happen in America, or around the globe, in the next 100 years. There might be much more shaking to come. But if our hope isn't set on our earthly nation, we will be okay.

Father, thank you that you have given me citizenship in your divine kingdom. I can rest when everything is shaking in my earthly country because it will never shake in my eternal one. There is no king like you in all the earth!

The Gift of Song

Praise the Lord!
Sing to the Lord a new song,
his praise in the assembly of the godly!
PSALM 149:1 ESV

Some of us are singers and some aren't. Some have been given a pitch-perfect voice, and others are embarrassed to sing too loudly for fear that hearers will cringe. Regardless of which camp you land in, God still gives you the gift of song.

All throughout Scripture we are encouraged to sing to God... a *new* song. He wants us to sing a song that hasn't been written by someone else, but one that is sung from our heart to his. Singing to God is an act of worship that delights God regardless of your vocal ability.

Father, help me worship you in song. I know that I alone can give you my voice of praise and worship. I thank you that you will encourage me as I sing about who you are and all you have done.

Parental Words

You are precious in my eyes,
and honored, and I love you.
ISAIAH 43:4 ESV

Parental words carry much power. If life-giving, those words help us face our greatest fears with added strength. We feel as if we can take on the world. The converse can be true as well. If the words we heard from our parents were full of defeat and discouragement, it might be hard to silence those words when we are trying to conquer obstacles.

For a child of God, there is a parental voice that carries more weight and power than that of our earthly parents. Being born of his will and not just the will of our parents, we have a truly supreme parent in God. So, receive his words of life to you. Know that you are precious to your Daddy and he loves you.

Father, help me to receive and not doubt your love today. I thank you that it will be my strength. With your words, I can walk in confidence and not shame.

Wash Away Sin

"Already you are clean because of the word that I have spoken to you."
JOHN 15:3 ESV

There are many options for trying to get stains out of clothes. Some will come out with a simple wash in the machine. Others require a special soaking product, and still others can be removed by scrubbing the fabric repeatedly. But have you ever had a stain that couldn't be removed? After you tried everything, you had to accept the fact that the stain was there to stay.

As Christians, we can become stained by the world through our own sin. Many of us try to use every method under the sun to feel clean again, but God's solution is simple. When you come to him in repentance, he himself will make you clean.

God, give me the grace to resist other methods
and simply enjoy your spoken word that alone can make me clean.

Trouble

The righteous person faces many troubles,
but the Lord comes to the rescue each time.

PSALM 34:19 NLT

Jesus, knowing exactly what his disciples needed to hear before he died, gave them lots of counsel. He knew they did not fully understand that he was getting ready to suffer. He wanted to make sure their theology accepted that even in the life of a believer—even in *his* life—suffering would be included. They would not be immune to it.

Indeed we will have troubles of many kinds, but we shouldn't be dismayed or surprised by them. God has not forgotten us or forsaken us. It is simply part of living here on earth. We might see dimly now, but God *did* overcome evil, and we will see his completed work in all its glory when we stand in his presence.

Thank you, Lord, that you come to my rescue in times of trouble. Help me endure to the end.

Not of This World

"My kingdom does not belong to this world."
JOHN 18:36 NCV

If you consume a regular diet of nightly news, it might be easy for you to become depressed. Wickedness seems to prevail, and some of the most heinous crimes continue to be committed. There are stories of corruption in our government and schools: institutions that are meant to be a stabilizing force in our communities.

Jesus makes it clear that we won't see his kingdom fully expressed here on earth. He is building a kingdom that cannot be shaken, but it isn't our government or our current social institutions. We might see little flickers of godliness in these places, but they are not his kingdom. His kingdom is coming and it will never end.

Father, thank you that your kingdom will be altogether different from what I see now. Give me eyes that are fixed on the day you set up your kingdom on earth, so I won't be discouraged by what is happening on the earth today.

In the Love of God

Keep yourselves in God's love as you wait for the Lord Jesus Christ
with his mercy to give you life forever.
JUDE 1:21 NCV

It's a simple but profound admonition. "Keep yourselves in God's love." What does it mean to keep yourself in God's love? Perhaps it's easier to picture what it doesn't mean. A heart that isn't in God's love is a heart that is accusatory and angry. When it sees calamity or suffering, instead of trusting that God is still love, it accuses him of being cruel and distant.

Nothing delights God more than a heart of faith that says, "Despite what I might see or experience, I still believe that you are a God of love." Our temptation will be to leave the love of God when we face hardship. That is why we are admonished to keep ourselves there, even if it takes all of our strength to do so.

Jesus, come what may, help me to never leave your love.
Give me the child-like trust I need to keep myself in your love.

Becoming Childlike

*"Truly I tell you, unless you change and become like little children,
you will never enter the kingdom of heaven."*
MATTHEW 18:3 NIV

Much of our childhood is spent preparing to be adults. Our parents wouldn't have been doing their jobs well if they encouraged us to remain like children. Instead, they spent hours training us to be successful adults.

God's job as our Father is different. In our spiritual journey, he doesn't want us to become like adults. If we do, we have to fight to become like children again. What is it about children that we need to become like them in our faith? It would appear to be their humility. Children aren't arrogant or self-sufficient: they happily receive provision from their parents. God beckons us to resist proud, adult-like tendencies and happily submit to his leadership and provision.

Jesus, help me become like a child so I might enter into your kingdom.

Not Worth Comparing

I consider that our present sufferings are not worth comparing
with the glory that will be revealed in us.
ROMANS 8:18 NIV

Are you suffering today? Is this a week of suffering or an entire season? The disciples that have gone before us, even those who walked with Jesus himself, all suffered: some as martyrs unto death, some watching their loved ones die, and others being shunned from their families because of their faith.

Paul knew suffering intimately, so his words should be of great courage to you. Our current suffering isn't even worth comparing to the glory that will be revealed. That glory of his coming kingdom will be so glorious that your current trial will pale in comparison. Find courage to keep pressing on, knowing that there is a glory that will far surpass your current pain.

Jesus, give me the hope I need to keep persevering for that day when I will never suffer again.

Rejoice in Suffering?

> We can rejoice, too, when we run into problems and trials,
> for we know that they help us develop endurance.
>
> ROMANS 5:3 NLT

God clearly tells us there is more to do in our sufferings than suffer. He calls us to rejoice. Thankfully, we immediately get a picture of what we are to be rejoicing about. God allows suffering for many different reasons—most of which we won't necessarily understand in this age. But one that we might be able to wrap our minds around is that suffering produces something good: endurance. Endurance is what allows us to go further than we once did.

Those who endure well are those who have suffered well. Endurance grows through trial and tribulation—not when things are easy. Let's not despise our trials; let's thank God that they are producing great endurance in us that will lead to character and hope.

Jesus, I thank you that my suffering isn't for nothing. I am growing in endurance as I suffer. Please help me remember that you give abundantly in all circumstances, not just when things are going well.

Feeding on Faithfulness

Trust in the Lord, and do good;
Dwell in the land, and feed on His faithfulness.
PSALM 37:3 NKJV

The person who trusts in the Lord has a beautiful life. Our trust in him alleviates all the natural tensions of our daily lives. We can be at peace knowing God will faithfully care for all of our needs. Our responsibility is just to do what is good in the land, rest in Christ, and enjoy the faithfulness of our Heavenly Father.

We simply must feed on his provisional care. When we meditate on his faithfulness, our stresses will be relieved, and we will enter a state of rest that can only be known by the true believer.

Lord, give me the ability to rest in you. Help me to look for opportunities to do good on this earth, and then to simply feel the peace of your faithful hand as I live for you.

Not without Hope

We were given this hope when we were saved. (If we already have something, we don't need to hope for it. But if we look forward to something we don't yet have, we must wait patiently and confidently.)

ROMANS 8:24-25 NLT

When you chose to trust God with your life, you did it in hope. No one gives their life to God expecting or hoping in nothing. You hope that the new life he gives you will be better than your present life. You hope that you will one day see him face to face. You hope that he will take your life and use it for his glory.

As Paul articulates, for something to be truly hoped for, we cannot already possess it. If we have it, then there is no need to hope for it. True hope rests in the belief and trust that something will come to pass. This isn't foolishness; it is Biblical. Have you grown weary in hoping? Approach God again, in the same hope you had when you were first saved.

Jesus, will you give me the courage to hope in what I do not already possess?

Continual Intercession

Who can say God's people are guilty? No one, because Christ Jesus died, but he was also raised from the dead, and now he is on God's right side, appealing to God for us.
ROMANS 8:34 NCV

Did you grow up with parents that prayed for you? Some of the most comforting words a child can ever hear are a parent's prayers. Not all of us had parents that prayed. Furthermore, some of those parents that once prayed may have gone on to heaven.

Take heart. There is still one who is praying. Perhaps your earthly parents aren't praying. That's alright. Someone who will always have the Father's ear is continually making intercession for you as he sits by God. His name is Jesus, and your name is written on the palm of his hand.

Jesus, thank you for your continual intercession over my life. I am so grateful for your perfect love and care of me. Help me to believe that you know what is best for me, and you will plead my case before the Father.

Strong Faith

Faith comes from what is heard, and what is heard comes though the words of Christ.
ROMANS 10:17 NRSV

Who are your heroes of the faith? What are some of the distinctions about them that you notice? People who have a deep faith in God are inspiring to us all. They remind us that no trial can consume us, that God is still there even when he seems distant. They seem unwavering in their walk when our feet feel unsteady.

Where does their faith come from? According to this verse, faith is grown largely from hearing the Word of Christ. It is hard to believe in promises that you don't even know exist. It is hard to trust in God's attributes and character if you haven't seen them yourself in Scripture. Don't forsake time in God's Word. Your faith will grow from hearing and believing it.

Father, thank you that faith comes from hearing your Word.
Give me perseverance to hear and study your Word regularly so that my faith is not weak.

Near to the Brokenhearted

The Lord is near to the brokenhearted,
and saves the crushed in spirit.
PSALM 34:18 NRSV

Have you ever been brokenhearted? What broke your heart? Was it a person? A circumstance that you couldn't change? Being brokenhearted is no small thing. It is not mere discouragement; it is severe pain. Pain that is hard to bounce back or recover from. There is little that can be done for those who are truly brokenhearted. And sometimes those who are very close get pushed away.

There is one who is allowed to go near a brokenhearted person: one that is not put off by rejection or grief. Isn't it a marvelous truth that the Lord is able to draw near to the brokenhearted. He is not kept at bay like others might be. This is because he alone is fully equipped to bear their pain. Are you brokenhearted or trying to comfort one who is? Go to God. He is already nearer to you than you realize.

Father, thank you that you are near to the brokenhearted.
Your nearness is what is needed more than anything else.

Superhuman Expectations

May He give you the power to accomplish all the good things your faith prompts you to do.
2 THESSALONIANS 1:11 NLT

God isn't asking you to be superhuman. Perhaps others are. Perhaps there are expectations placed on you that are unreasonable or unattainable. If that is the case, please don't exhaust yourself trying to be someone that you can't be.

God knows your frame. He is your maker and your designer. He didn't give you an indestructible body like his. He made you from dust and you will one day return to being dust. He knows that you are innately weak and your body will fail. This shouldn't discourage you. Take great heart that he doesn't expect you to be or act like him. He will give you an indestructible resurrected body one day. Today, your frame is one that will return to dust. This is a hopeful truth because it allows you to draw your strength from the one who is *superhuman*. His strength is yours when you lean on him.

Jesus, help me not despise or cover my weakness. Rather, give me the grace to enjoy and receive your strength. I am not superhuman, and I gladly rely on your strength to help me do all the things you have purposed for me to do.

Steadfast Love

As high as the heavens are above the earth,
so great is his steadfast love toward those who fear him.
PSALM 103:11 ESV

Let's take a moment to contemplate *steadfast love*. Steadfast love is steady. It doesn't get offended easily. It can weather incredible relational strain. It can handle faithlessness. It won't quit even when the recipient's love has grown cold.

This is steadfast love. And this is how God describes his love toward his children.

He promises fidelity and faithful love even when you aren't faithful to him. If you run from him, upon your repentance he stands ready to accept you and pour more of his steadfast love upon you. He won't charge you for it or remind you of your weakness. He will simply strengthen you.

Father, thank you that you are different than I am. Thank you that your love is pure and steadfast. Help me to believe and trust you for that today.

Worthless Things

Turn my eyes from looking at worthless things;
and give me life in your ways.
PSALM 119:37 ESV

Does social media call your name throughout your day? There is no doubt that it can be a gift from God. It can hold encouragement for you that you otherwise would not have seen. It can alert you to a prayer need that is urgent. And it can remind you of a loved one's birthday.

There is also no denying that it can be a colossal waste of time. There are worthless things all over our social media outlets. We are not alone in our struggle to resist looking at those things. Even in the days before Christ, people were tempted to waste their time on worthless cares. God wants us to have life, and that comes as we walk in his ways.

Father, please forgive me for the time I have wasted in idleness. Thank you that you promise life in your ways. Help me turn away from worthless things and abide in you today.

Do Not Grow Weary

Let us not grow weary of doing good, for in due season we will reap, if we do not give up.
GALATIANS 6:9 ESV

A time-tested principle is that you reap what you sow. Apart from any environmental upheaval, if you plant corn, you will reap corn. If you plant soy beans, you will reap soy beans. You can confidently sow a row of spinach and not be weary of cauliflower growing in its place. Cauliflower won't grow because you didn't sow cauliflower seeds.

That same principle applies to sowing seeds of goodness. If you sow seeds of goodness like forgiveness, gentleness, and honesty, you are guaranteed to reap the fruit of those seeds. There is one trick—don't give up. Don't plan to reap something that you just started sowing. Maybe you will see fruit immediately from the good seeds you planted, but in most cases, it takes years. Rest assured, you will eventually reap the seeds of goodness if you don't give up.

Lord, help me not grow weary in doing good.
Give me long term vision that doesn't get discouraged in short term losses.

September

Come, let us all unite to sing, God is love;
Let heav'n and earth their praises ring, God is love;
Let ev'ry soul from sin awake,
Each in his heart sweet music make,
And sing with us for Jesus' sake,
For God is love.

God is love! God is love!
Come let us all unite to sing
That God is love.

How happy is our portion here, God is love;
His promises our spirits cheer, God is love;
He is our sun and shield by day,
Our help, our hope, our strength, and stay,
He will be with us all the way,
Our God is love.

God Is Love
ANONYMOUS

A Basket Case

"I took the load off their shoulders;
I let them put down their baskets."
PSALM 81:6 NCV

People in developing countries typically have few options when a heavy load of some kind must be moved. In Africa, a tribal woman can carry up to 70% of her body weight on the top of her head. Physical burdens are—yes—burdensome and require strength and stamina.

Spiritual and emotional burdens are the same. The heaviness and fatigue of the soul can bring depression and even a loss of hope. There is great news, however! We have a burden bearer—one who is well equipped and ready to remove our hands from our heavy load! Our responsibility is to let him do it. Put all of your concerns, worries, fears, and doubts into God's mighty basket and let him haul it away! You don't have to be a basket case!

Lord, today I'm placing all of my concerns into your ample basket. I release it to your care.
As you solve all these issues, let me know how to proceed one step at a time.
Thank you for being my burden bearer!

Are You Shining?

"You are the light of the world. A city set on a hill cannot be hidden."
MATTHEW 5:14 ESV

Lights from major cities like Los Angeles, Nashville, and Atlanta can be seen from space. In fact, their brilliance increases 50% more during the holiday season! These cities simply cannot be hidden.

As believers, we are to be a light, shining for all to see. If there ever was a time in history where the beacon of light needed to illumine the darkness, it is now! We dare not hide behind the façade of political correctness and fear, but rather speak and live in the luminance of Christ's truth. We have the light of the world living in us and we know the truth that sets us free.

Lord, shine through me this day. Give me courage to speak and live according to your Word, no matter what the world may say. I want your glow to radiate through me.

Bad News

They will have no fear of bad news;
their hearts are steadfast, trusting in the Lord.
PSALM 112:7 NIV

In this age of technology, we can be inundated with happenings from around the world. News is always at our fingertips—and often it's not good. Sometimes we are waiting for the personal, life-changing kind of news: the medical report, the upshot of the job interview, the test score. Our fear is that the result will not be what we hope.

Psalm 112 tells us that we do not have to fear bad news! If our hearts are righteous, we are steadfast and secure. In spite of any alarming information coming our way, we can be at peace because we are safe in God's hands.

I am so thankful, Lord, that even though bad news assaults and sometimes awaits, I do not need to fear even the scariest of prospects. I am safe and secure in you no matter the situation.

Bloom Where You Are Planted

"They are those who, hearing the word, hold it fast in an honest and good heart, and bear fruit with patience."

LUKE 8:15 ESV

Most of us want to make a significant mark somewhere in our lifetime. It's comforting to believe that the routine of our ordinary lives is merely preparation for the really big assignment that surely is just around the corner. You know, the lofty thing, the high calling, the noble assignment that undoubtedly is directly ahead.

Then one day in a moment of quiet, the Lord whispers, "This is it. What you are doing is what I've called you to do. Do your work, raise your kids, love your neighbor, serve people, seek me first, and everything in your heart you long for will be fulfilled. Be faithful right where I've put you. You don't need to accomplish great things for me. Just be."

Lord, I so long for significance. I want my life to matter. Help me to understand that it's not what I do for you that is important... it's whose I am and who I am. Help me to be faithful in the assignment you have given me right now.

Blackbird Bluff

Stay alert! Watch out for your great enemy, the devil. He prowls around like a roaring lion, looking for someone to devour. Stand firm against him, and be strong in your faith.

1 PETER 5:8-9 NLT

In the parking lot of a lovely little park, a sleek blackbird demanded attention. He was busy pecking at a small wad of bread, surely enjoying an unexpected treat. A much larger blackbird circled him menacingly—moving in closer, then hopping back. You could almost hear his bird voice squawking, "Drop it buddy, and I mean now!" The smaller bird seemed completely oblivious. He was not in the least frightened, and he continued to enjoy his dinner. After a moment, the bully bird backed off. He was suddenly the same size as the other bird. He had puffed his feathers out in an attempt to look big and scary. The smaller bird knew he was a phony and paid him no mind.

The Bible describes our enemy, Satan, as a roaring lion, prowling around looking for someone to devour. A lion that roars is not to be feared because he has given his presence away, allowing his prey time to escape. When we are in tune with God, we don't need to fear Satan's tactics. We will hear the roar a mile away and take appropriate action to see to his defeat. Satan's roar is not to be feared because compared to God he is all blackbird bluff. Let's pay him no mind!

Lord, give me discernment so that I can recognize the enemy's tactics and lies. Thank you for giving me the victory as I take my stand against his wiles.

Bridging the Gap

*Faith is the confidence that what we hope for will actually happen;
it gives us assurance about things we cannot see.*
HEBREWS 11:1 NLT

Do you ever feel like there is an enormous gap between what you *know* to be true in God's Word and what you *feel* to be true? Our feelings are so fickle. They fluctuate depending on our circumstances, much as our moods change with the weather. The good news is that they don't change facts! God promises strength, wisdom, peace, hope, direction, comfort, forgiveness, courage, eternal life, and so much more. These are unchangeable—they are written in stone.

How do we move from the tyranny of emotions to the confidence of faith? We must determine to believe what God says instead of what our emotions say, and then declare his promises aloud! Then we do it again and again and again until faith rises and bridges the gap.

Lord, your Word is true and I know it. Right now, I feel so alone and frightened even though I know you promise never to leave me or forsake me. I choose to believe the truth. Help me now by the power of your Spirit.

But Dust

For He Himself knows our frame;
He is mindful that we are but dust.

PSALM 103:14 NASB

A story is told of a little boy who heard his pastor reading Psalm 103 from the pulpit. When he read verse fourteen, the boy leaned over to his mother and whispered, "Mommy, what is butt dust?" That aside, it is rather disconcerting to note that God refers to us as nothing more than dust. He says, "Our days on earth are like grass; like wildflowers, we bloom and die. The wind blows, and we are gone—as though we had never been here."

The truth is that we are incredibly important dust to God. Listen to the litany of all God has done for the millions of tiny specks on this earth. He has forgiven our sins, rescued us from punishment, healed our diseases, filled our life with good things, and given us his righteousness. Merely dirt? Well, he knows our frame, because he framed us! He knows we are weak and mortal and without his powerful hand upon us, we would be irrecoverably destroyed.

Oh Lord, on days when I feel insignificant, help me remember the amazing expressions of love you have lavished on me. You valued me enough to die for me and some day will exchange this body of dust for a glorious eternal one!

Clay Pots

You, Lord, are our Father.
We are the clay, you are the potter;
we are all the work of your hand.
ISAIAH 64:8 NIV

There are many types of pottery—from basic earthenware used for mundane tasks to lovely, decorative pieces that adorn someone's mantelpiece. It is interesting to note that God uses this imagery all the way from Genesis to Revelation. He is the artist (potter); we are the clay. The potter has absolute power to create exactly according to his wish; the pot has no say.

There are times when we are not happy with the vessel the potter has fashioned. We'd rather be the vase on the mantelpiece that is used to hold a beautiful bouquet. The truth is, the vessel itself is not what gives it worth—as beautiful as it may be. The value lies in the contents.

Lord, forgive me for being discontented with this vessel you created. I know that outward appearance is meaningless compared to the inward glory of Christ's presence. Shine through this vessel; use me as you wish, and let the world know who you are.

*E*at for Life

Man does not live by bread alone, but man lives by everything that proceeds
out of the mouth of the Lord.
DEUTERONOMY 8:3 NASB

It isn't often that we err on the side of eating too little! Hunger pangs, boredom, anxiety, even depression can propel us to the refrigerator! There is one kind of food that we can ingest without restraint—the meat of the Word.

The Scriptures are our spiritual food: a veritable banquet laid out for our enjoyment. The Word will nourish, guide, comfort, convict, keep us from sinning, and satisfy every hungry, thirsty soul. Read it and remember that as one weakens physically without regular meals, so the soul will become impoverished without habitual intake of the Word. Eat for life!

Lord, thank you for your Word that nourishes and strengthens me and gives me tools for life.
Increase my love and desire for it each day.

Necessary Instrument

All Scripture is inspired by God and profitable for teaching, for reproof, for correction, for training in righteousness; so that the man of God may be adequate, equipped for every good work.
2 TIMOTHY 3:16-17 NASB

Most tasks require a tool. In daily living it may be a broom, drill, lawnmower, hose, bucket, hammer, or parachute! It takes something to accomplish something.

In our spiritual lives we need tools as well. God never intended us to struggle along without the necessary instruments for success. Scripture, breathed by God, is the divine workshop complete with resources for the taking. Its purpose is to teach, correct, and convict so that we can live wisely! Are we reading, studying, and hiding the words in our hearts, or are we empty, dry, and ill-equipped for the life he has called us to? Open the Bible and ask God to help you implement the truths found there.

Lord, I so often feel ineffective and inadequate in my Christian life and fail frequently. It just seems too difficult at times. I know your Word is a lamp to guide my feet and a light for my path. Help me remain in it.

Faith's End

"If you have faith like a grain of mustard seed, you will say to this mountain,
'Move from here to there,' and it will move, and nothing will be impossible for you."
MATTHEW 17:20 ESV

A teacher is about to illustrate the meaning of faith. He instructs a child to stand with his back toward him, close his eyes and fall backwards into his outstretched arms. The child needs a great measure of faith in that teacher. Is he trustworthy? Squeezing his eyes shut, the child falls backwards and is caught by the teacher who then explains how we similarly need to completely trust God.

Trusting God with such abandon is not always easy. It means we are at peace with whatever the outcome may be. Often we pray earnestly for a specific answer and we think that the outcome of that prayer reveals the measure of our faith. We long for healing, provision, a job, that miracle. But the end result of our faith is none of those things—it's the salvation of our souls! Don't over analyze your amount of faith. Stay in the Word and your faith will grow. In the meantime, fall into God's arms with abandon; he will catch you!

Jesus, thank you for granting me the saving faith that resulted in the salvation of my soul. Like a child, I fall into your arms with joy.

Held Together

He is before all things, and in him all things hold together.
COLOSSIANS 1:17 NIV

Often life seems to be a conglomeration of unrelated activities and we feel pulled in a thousand directions simultaneously. Loose ends, unfinished business, and to-do lists leave us feeling a day late and a dollar short. Frustration, discouragement, and anxiety often overwhelm. The apostle Paul must have experienced something similar when he was on a ship headed to Jerusalem to be tried in court. An enormous storm raged. In an effort to survive, the sailors wrapped ropes around the body of the ship to keep it from falling apart. God promised Paul that all would survive the wreck, and they did!

What an amazing truth it is to know that it is not our job to hold our lives together. Our responsibility is to submit our to-do list to God, bow to his will and let him hold it all together. He is the rope that holds us fast.

Lord, thank you that you are the glue that keeps me together. Today as I face the impossible list of my responsibilities, I submit to your will and ask you to hold everything in place.

How Do I Love Thee?

This is love: that we walk in obedience to his commands.
As you have heard from the beginning, his command is that you walk in love.
2 JOHN 6 NIV

Love is probably the most overused, over romanticized word in the human language. We fall in love, we love pizza, and we love our pet cat. Scripture tells us that we are supposed to love God. How do we love an invisible being?

In 1 John 2:3-5, John defines love for God by saying that the proof of our love for him is our obedience. We don't need to search for an elusive emotion. We just need to obey.

My prayer today, Lord, is that you will give me a heart of obedience.
Teach me to do your will and give me a new love for your Word.

Idols of the Heart

Son of man, these leaders have set up idols in their hearts. They have embraced things that will make them fall into sin. Why should I listen to their requests?
EZEKIEL 14:3 NLT

God had a strong message for Israel. He told Ezekiel that he would not entertain the people's requests because they had set up idols in their hearts, which separated them from him. He wasn't talking about physical objects, but something of a different dimension. What did he mean? Possessions, prestige, position, power? Self, entertainment, rules, religion? Internet, sports, hobbies? Whatever consumes our time could become an idol of the heart.

Maybe it's time do to some soul searching. What squanders our time, our thoughts, and dictates our priorities? Are we embracing things that will lead us into sin? At times we wonder why God doesn't seem to be listening to our prayers. It's possible that there's an idol in the way.

O God, show me where I have allowed activities and attitudes to become idols in my heart. Don't let me get by with foolish notions or be consumed by anything that would lead me into sin. I don't want any idols in my heart. I want to worship you only.

Joy

Do not grieve, for the joy of the Lord is your strength.
NEHEMIAH 8:10 NIV

Joy is not necessarily happiness. Happiness is dependent on circumstances; joy is not. Happiness is fleeting; joy is constant. Happiness disappears when trials come; joy grows through troubles. Good times bring happiness and laughter; difficulties bring sorrow and grief, but joy resides beneath.

Joy is not an emotion that can be fabricated or faked. It is a deep-seated sense that all things are well because God is in charge. Joy is expressed in praise, song, laughter, a peaceful countenance, a light in the eyes, or a serenity that belies any adversity. It is the substance of the soul that holds us together as we trust in God, who does all things well. Jesus wants our joy to be full!

Thank you, Jesus, for the joy that gives me strength. I choose today to fill my mind with truth, to think about those things that are praiseworthy, and to trust you fully.
With a thankful heart, I choose joy.

_____

_____

_____

_____

_____

_____

_____

_____

Kept

We know that anyone born of God does not continue to sin;
the One who was born of God keeps them safe, and the evil one cannot harm them.
1 JOHN 5:1 NIV

Little Peter's legs are pumping as he heads toward the road. Mom yells, "Stop, stop!" If he is an obedient child, he will immediately put on the brakes. She protects him from danger, but his safety depends on his compliance.

In a similar way, God's Word is clear about what he expects of us. His purpose is to keep us from harm. If we have submitted ourselves to God, we will obey. However, God's involvement with our obedience is profound. He not only gives us the strength but the will to obey him, and then he goes a step further. He keeps us! God protects us from the evil that surrounds us and the sin we could easily fall into. This does not mean we will never be tempted, suffer, or go through hardship. It simply means we can persevere, kept by God's power.

Lord, how grateful I am for your keeping power. Thank you for the dangers you have saved me from that I'm not even aware of! Today I nestle into the safety of your protection.

Light at the End of the Tunnel

"I am the light of the world.
Whoever follows me will never walk in darkness,
but will have the light of life."
JOHN 8:12 NIV

There's an old adage dating back to the 1800s we've probably all quoted: "There is a light at the end of the tunnel." Translated: "Hang on. The end of whatever difficulty you are in is in sight!" However, there are times when there probably is no positive ending to be had, and there is no light at the end of our tunnel. What then?

Jesus is light and he dwells in us. We are surrounded by his presence no matter where we are. He is behind us, before us, to the right and the left, above and beneath. We are cocooned in his presence and do not walk in darkness. He is our light. No more walking through dark tunnels with only a spot of hope at the end. We walk through our tunnels blazing with the light of Jesus!

Lord, I acknowledge that you, the light of the world, live in me. I do not need to fear the darkness or the outcome. Help me remember that the light of your presence never leaves me.

Never Give Up!

I call on you, my God, for you will answer me;
turn your ear to me and hear my prayer.
PSALM 17:6 NIV

Jesus taught that we should pray and never give up! He told of a widow who was being mistreated by an enemy and came to a judge hoping for a settlement. The judge, who didn't give a rip about God or people, finally relented and reluctantly handed down a decision! Why? Because the widow approached him again and again and again.

God will never put us off or turn us away, but will respond quickly. Our *quickly* may not be the same as God's though. Many times he waits to answer for a variety of reasons. Perhaps the most important reason is that in the waiting, we will learn to seek God, to keep crying out to him and trusting him against all odds. But pray we must. And then pray some more!

Lord, help me to persevere in prayer even when you don't seem to be responding.
I know that you are working behind the scenes and your answer will come at exactly
the right time. I lift up my need to you once again and will trust you while I wait.

Perennials

*As the soil makes the sprout come up and a garden causes seeds to grow,
so the Sovereign Lord will make righteousness and praise spring up before all nations.*
ISAIAH 61:11 NIV

Jesus loved to tell stories about farmers and fields. We are familiar with his teaching on the seeds, the weeds, the pruning. Have you ever considered the perennial plant? It courageously weathers the winters and returns to grow and bloom. Some are garden bullies—they can rush over another plant without so much as an "excuse me." If you're not careful, your entire garden can be overrun by one aggressive plant.

In our lives, there are things that in themselves are not wrong. But when they are allowed to take over, they become a huge detriment to our spiritual growth. How much time do we spend on useless activities—computer games, Facebook, talk shows, television, movies? Maybe it's time to reign in the perennials in our lives, remembering our time on this earth is limited.

Lord, it's true. I squander too much time on things that don't really matter. Give me the discipline to weed out the perennials in my life and use my time for your glory.

Sins of Omission

To one who knows the right thing to do and does not do it, to him it is sin.
JAMES 4:17 NASB

A young mom and her kids would often bike past an older lady resting in a chair in front of a shabby looking mobile home. Something stirred in the mom's heart, and she knew the woman needed the Gospel. She fully intended to stop by for a visit. Procrastination won out until it was too late. One day the woman's lot was completely empty… there was no sign of life and only a patch on the ground where the home had been.

Sins of commission are fairly obvious; those of omission are easier to rationalize away. The Holy Spirit prompts us to share Christ, or cut off a relationship, or invite the neighbor for dinner, but we're too harried, too consumed by our own plans. In our hearts, we know what we are to do, but somehow the commitment to obey is not there. Let's change that. Let's heed the gentle voice of the Holy Spirit.

Jesus, I confess that I am guilty of sins of omission. I simply do not obey your nudging and then justify my delaying. Quicken my spirit not only to hear your voice clearer but to have a passion for obedience.

Starting Over

Praise the Lord!
Oh, give thanks to the Lord, for He is good!
For His mercy endures forever.
PSALM 106:1 NKJV

Have you ever wished you could have a do-over? It would be so great to turn back the clock, reverse a decision, and do it differently. There is so much more wisdom in looking back! Yes, there are some things we can do over, like tweak the recipe or rip the seam, but most often, the important big decisions can't be changed.

Except when it comes to spiritual things. God tells us that we can start over every morning because his mercies will be there. Whatever went awry the day before, whatever mess we made from poor choices, we can begin the next day with a completely clean slate! There does not need to be any carryover of yesterday's mistakes. Our part in the transaction may require repentance of sin or forgiving someone, perhaps even ourselves. Bathed in his mercies, we can begin each day squeaky clean!

Lord, I am so grateful that your love and your mercies never end.
You extend them to me brand new every morning! Great is your faithfulness!

_____

_____

_____

_____

_____

_____

_____

SEPTEMBER 22

The Deliverance Trilogy

He has delivered us from such a deadly peril, and he will deliver us again.
On him we have set our hope that he will continue to deliver us.

2 CORINTHIANS 1:10 NIV

Deliverance. What a marvelous word. It is liberation, emancipation, freedom, rescue. Anyone who has experienced the antonyms of any of these words knows the exhilaration of deliverance. Think of the demon-possessed man Jesus saved. Homeless, naked, living in a cemetery. He was guarded, shackled, chained, and completely controlled by an evil spirit. At Jesus' word, he was set free!

We, too, are in need of deliverance. Bound by sin and needing a Savior, we were delivered. When we battle temptation and confusion and our faith falters, we need to be delivered again. As adversity finds its way to our doorstep and difficulties overwhelm, we have the hope that God will continue to deliver us: past, present, and future.

Lord, I am so grateful that you are a God of deliverances—not just once, but as often as I need it. Help me to set my hope on you. Help me know you are faithful to your Word and will continue to rescue me.

279

The Divine Song

Shout with joy to the Lord, all the earth; burst into songs and make music.
Make music to the Lord with harps, with harps and the sound of singing.
Blow the trumpets and the sheep's horns; shout for joy to the Lord the King.

PSALM 98:4-6 NCV

The gift of music is surely from the heart of God to his creation. Melodies, harmonies, rhythms, and the infinite configuration of notes and styles inspire, soothe, and stimulate according to their genre. Mortal music is a wonder. Can you imagine the incredible beauty of heavenly instruments?

Keep the beauty of heavenly song in your mind, and then contemplate the fact that God surrounds us with songs of deliverance and even sings over us with melodies of victory! The purpose of this music is to hide us in his love, protect us from trouble, calm our fears, and give us the victory over the enemy. We are cocooned in the divine song. Let's sing our joyful praise back to God, for he is worthy!

Oh God, how I love you for surrounding me with joyful songs of victory.
Today I will lift up a melody of praise to you.

SEPTEMBER 24

The Vine

*"I am the vine, you are the branches; he who abides in Me and I in him,
he bears much fruit, for apart from Me you can do nothing."*
JOHN 15:5 NASB

A mother often has a difficult time letting her children grow up and fly the nest. She has given so much of herself, her time, and her energy to their raising that their absence leaves a hollow place—a gaping hole. In the serving, she has found fulfillment, nourishment, and meaning. Her fountainhead of joy and life seems to have been sealed off.

This dilemma begs an explanation, and Jesus does it well in this verse. He reminds us that he is the vine. We are the branches that must remain in the vine in order to receive sustenance. If we are attached to anything other than him—children, spouse, job, ministry—we will wither away and die because those resources are merely human. We must stay connected to Jesus. Without the life of the vine flowing through us, we will bear no fruit.

Lord, you are my source. I choose to disconnect from any person or activity I have used to gain a sense of worth and accomplishment and attach to you only. You are my everything.

Three Things We Can Know

We know that we belong to God, but the Evil One controls the whole world. We also know that the Son of God has come and has given us understanding so that we can know the True One. And our lives are in the True One and in his Son, Jesus Christ. He is the true God and the eternal life.

1 JOHN 5:19-20 NCV

We live in a world where absolutes seem to be a thing of the past. Many in our culture believe there are no absolutes because of the variables of background, ethnicity, and religion. Unfortunately, there are people in our churches who vacillate, succumbing to the influences of society. Grey areas have emerged where black and white should be.

John clearly states that we *can* know absolute truth. We know that God keeps us safe from sin and the evil one, we know we belong to God, and we can know the True One. It's all right there in God's Word.

Lord, in this world of changing ideas and fluid belief systems, help me cling to the truth of your Word. Thank you that I can know I belong to you and you to me. Help me to resist the societal trends that pull me away from your truth.

Unchanging

Jesus Christ is the same yesterday and today and forever.
HEBREWS 13:8 NASB

You may have heard the saying, "There is nothing permanent except change." The word *change* itself can evoke a number of responses: fear, dread, worry, sadness, or loss. It can produce a grief of sorts as we realize things will never be the same. There is safety in the familiar: a sense of continuity with the flow of life that is unsettling when altered.

Relationships change, friends move, loved ones pass on, culture shifts, aging takes place, and it can be painful. God knows this. He makes sure his Word contains the one assurance we are desperate to know. He never changes. He doesn't get old, or move away, or busy himself elsewhere. He is the same God who created the world, sent his Son to redeem us from our sin, and gave his Holy Spirit to be with us always. No matter how our lives change from day to day, we can bank on his constancy.

Jesus, I am so grateful to know that although my life continues to shift and change with each passing year, with you there is no variation. You will always be my savior, deliverer, helper, and friend. Thank you.

Waiting

Wait for the Lord;
Be strong, and let your heart take courage;
Yes, wait for the Lord!
PSALM 27:14 NASB

Is there anything positive to be said about waiting? Whether we are in line at the grocery store, stuck in traffic, or simply waiting for a package to arrive, it is part of our daily lives. Waiting seems like a colossal waste of time. And yet, God tells us specifically (35 times or so) we are to "wait for the Lord."

The concept of waiting on God seems to originate with the Psalmist. Perhaps it was because he was so often stuck in perilous situations and he knew his only hope was God. The kind of waiting he speaks of is not passive as though our spiritual lives are put on hold until God comes through with our request. It is an active display of faith as we lay down our desires, hopes, and dreams before the Lord and surrender to his will. In the waiting, he is perfecting our faith and building our character.

Oh Lord, how I loathe waiting. I am so impatient. God grant me the grace to humbly wait upon you as you conform me to your image. Your timing is best and I surrender to it.

Weak Strength

"My grace is sufficient for you, for my power is made perfect in weakness." Therefore I will boast all the more gladly about my weaknesses, so that Christ's power may rest on me.

2 CORINTHIANS 12:9 NIV

There's something inside of us that longs to be strong and self-sufficient. Don't we admire the woman who can raise children, work, volunteer, and yet appear put together? Even if people like that don't really exist, in our minds they do! We get impatient with our weakness and insufficiencies.

What a relief to know that God doesn't expect us to be strong! In fact, the apostle Paul said he delighted in his weaknesses, insults, hardships, persecution, and difficulties! God isn't looking for us to be strong. He's looking for us to turn to him in our weaknesses so his power can rest upon us! Let's start being grateful for our shortcomings and give God a chance to demonstrate his power!

Lord, I admit I am frail and flawed and so often come up short. I'm so thankful that this is not news to you. You are waiting for me to admit it and ask for your strength. I gratefully receive it.

Where Are You Looking?

Let your eyes look straight ahead;
fix your gaze directly before you.
PROVERBS 4:25 NIV

A stylish young lady is strolling along leisurely, texting with her friend. She glances up periodically to assess her location and then returns her gaze to the contraption she is holding. She senses a shadow looming and lifts her eyes, finding herself face-to-bark with a birch tree!

Keeping our spiritual eyes focused on what's ahead is even more important.

Often we look around, searching for other resources to meet our needs, to solve our problems, to give us direction instead of looking straight to Jesus. The amazing truth is that God is longing to make eye contact with us! We look to Jesus, he looks back, and when our eyes meet—we have indeed touched the divine.

Oh, God, help me fix my eyes on you. My gaze is apt to wander.
Thank you that as I look to you, you are looking right back at me.

Willing to Teach—Willing to Learn

Similarly, teach the older women to live in a way that honors God...These older women must train the younger women to love their husbands and their children, to live wisely and be pure, to work in their homes, to do good, and to be submissive to their husbands.

TITUS 2:3-5 NLT

Mothers and daughters have a complex relationship that gradually shifts until they become peers. Ahead of the daughter by years of experience, the mother has much to give. However, the daughter may pass through a season where she is not interested in any wisdom from mom and is unwilling to learn. And yet, here the apostle Paul writes that older women should teach the younger ones to live a godly life.

This admonition is two-fold and potentially problematic. First, the older women must live circumspectly before the Lord and then be willing to teach others. Secondly, the younger women must be willing to learn! Sometimes the youthful prefer to learn from their peer group, viewing the elders as somewhat outdated. Conversely, the older woman may feel disconnected and extinct herself. Let's overcome these hindrances and be women who are willing to teach and willing to learn!

Lord, help me to be willing to heed your instruction. I have much to give and much to learn from my sisters in Christ. Give me an opportunity today to put your Word into action!

October

Time is filled with swift transition—
Naught of earth unmoved can stand—
Build your hope on things eternal,
Hold to God's unchanging hand.

Trust in Him who will not leave you,
Whatsoever years may bring,
If by earthly friends forsaken,
Still more closely to Him cling.

When your journey is completed,
If to God you have been true,
Fair and bright the home in glory,
Your enraptured soul will view.

Hold to God's Unchanging Hand
By Jennie Wilson

The Complete Believer

For when the way is rough, your patience has a chance to grow. So let it grow, and don't try to squirm out of your problems. For when your patience is finally in full bloom, then you will be ready for anything, strong in character, full and complete.

JAMES 1:3-4 TLB

We all will see our fair share of hard times in this life. In the difficulties, we will develop and grow into believers that are complete—ready for anything.

God has a heavenly, eternal perspective and he is shaping us and preparing us for things that are greater than what we can imagine. If we will hold on and trust him, he will reveal to us a more beautiful purpose than we could have dreamed.

God, help me to trust you in all things, especially the hardships. Let me surrender myself to your process so that I can become full and complete—the kind of believer that you can use for your glory.

I Will Help You

I will instruct you and teach you in the way you should go;
I will counsel you with my loving eye on you.
PSALM 32:8 NIV

Every day we are faced with fear, but sometimes fear becomes so great it starts to control us. What if, instead of being paralyzed by our fears, we told God what we were afraid of? God promises that he will hold our hand, calm our fears, and help us through whatever we're facing.

We don't have to walk alone in fear—we can be strengthened by God's truth and helped by his power.

Lord, when fear starts to grip me and I become overwhelmed by everything I'm afraid of, I pray that you would give me the strength to tell you. I know that if I turn to you, you will hold my hand through it and help me find peace and power by your Holy Spirit.

Songs of Victory

You are my hiding place;
you protect me from trouble.
You surround me with songs of victory.
PSALM 32:7 NLT

Life can feel like a battle sometimes. From keeping up with busy schedules to making major decisions, we are met with challenges daily. Some days we just want to hide away for a while so we can recharge and refocus.

God is our hiding place—our protection and our rest. He walks with us through the battles of life and sings a song of victory over us. With Christ as our strength, we can not only make it through the battle, we can come out as joyful victors.

Lord, as I face the challenges in my daily life, help me run to you. As I hide myself in you, give me your peace, your rest, and your hope. I pray that I would enter my battles with confidence, knowing that you will give me the victory.

Refuge for the Questioning Soul

Trust in him at all times, you people;
pour out your hearts to him, for God is our refuge.

PSALM 62:8 NIV

There are questions that we long to have answered by God, and circumstances in our lives that leave us wondering about his goodness. As we pray, we try to rend the heavens for an answer that will make sense of our storm.

What God desires most isn't the soul with the answer—it's the one laid bare before him in a perfect dance of trust, belief, and raw vulnerability. In that moment of emptiness before your Maker, he will be your safe place. Pour out your heart to him and rest in his embrace because he is a refuge for even the most questioning soul.

God, I don't have answers for all of the deep questions, but I know that you are
a safe place for me to pour out my heart. I give you my questions and my fears,
and I say yes to the peace of your presence.

Waiting for the Promise

Your promises have been thoroughly tested,
and your servant loves them.
My eyes stay open through the watches of the night,
that I may meditate on your promises.
PSALM 119:140, 148 NIV

What has God promised you? Have you felt his promise through a certain Scripture? Or perhaps through words spoken over your life that cast a vision in your soul? When God promises something, it takes faith to believe that he will bring it to pass.

Years may go by from the moment of vision to the moment of fruition. The waiting can either be a time of bitterness, or it can be a time of great sweetness with the Lord as you grow in trust, faith, and praise.

Lord, I ask that you would grow my faith as I wait for the promises you've given me to come to pass. I surrender to your timetable, and I refuse to doubt your goodness.

For Us, Not Against Us

What, then, shall we say in response to these things? If God is for us, who can be against us?
ROMANS 8:31 NIV

God is for us. What a powerful idea that the God of the universe is *for* us. We sometimes buy into this untruthful image of God, depicting him as angry, distant, and condemning. But God is for us; he is not against us. His heart toward us has eternally been compassionate, loving, merciful, and tender.

God's desire for unhindered relationship with us is displayed impeccably by Christ—who laid everything down to fight for our hearts.

Heavenly Father, I pray that whenever I begin to feel as though you are against me, I would remember that it is the opposite that's true. You have been for me since the beginning. You are not against me; you are my friend. Thank you for your steadfast love and your unfailing mercy.

Comfort

Praise be to the God and Father of our Lord Jesus Christ, the Father of compassion and the God of all comfort, who comforts us in all our troubles, so that we can comfort those in any trouble with the comfort we ourselves receive from God.

2 CORINTHIANS 1:3-4 NIV

When we face trouble, God doesn't just watch us struggling from a distance. He is our comfort, our strength, and our hope. And as he comforts us, he also teaches us how to comfort others.

Whatever difficult thing we may have walked through, there is someone else who is walking through something very, very similar. Our experiences can be the one thing that keeps that person afloat during their hard time.

God, help me to be aware of the people in my life who are struggling. Help me to be someone who comforts others in their trials because I know the power of your comfort. Thank you for being a God who is not far off and for walking with me through every difficulty in my life.

Encouraged in Faith

When we get together, I want to encourage you in your faith,
but I also want to be encouraged by yours.
ROMANS 1:12 NLT

True, life giving friendship will be characterized by a mutual encouragement of faith in Christ. Have you ever had a friend who, after you've been with them, makes you want to know God more? A friend whose love for the Lord is infectious? That is the type of friendship that we should strive to surround ourselves with: the kind of friend who will point us to Christ and make us long for his presence.

True friendship results in true fellowship—a source of strength, community, and accountability.

God, surround me with friends who encourage me in my faith. Bring me friends who I can truly fellowship with, who will call me higher every time I am with them. Let me be an encouragement to the friends you've put in my life so that I can lead them closer to you.

Stronghold

The Lord is good,
A stronghold in the day of trouble;
And He knows those who trust in Him.
NAHUM 1:7 NKJV

God isn't only with us when our faith comes easy and our praise is unrestrained. Even in the day of trouble, God knows intimately those who trust him, and he is a stronghold for them.

Not only in catastrophe, but even in our moments of hidden weakness, God is our strength and our refuge. We can trust him and know that he is always good.

Thank you, Lord, that you are a source of strength for me even in my weakest moments. You remember my trust in you when I feel close to losing my faith. You do not forget me, and you are more than enough for me. You take my darkest hour and bring the light of your countenance to me.

The Power of Seeking

Even there you can look for the Lord your God,
and you will find him if you look for him with your whole being.

DEUTERONOMY 4:29 NCV

Do you have days when you feel empty, weary, and uninspired? Days when you feel you have nothing to give, even though there is no shortage of demand. You don't know how to fill back up; you only know that you need to.

The Lord says that if you look for him with your whole being, you will find him. God will not withhold himself from his child who asks. Even here, in this place of emptiness, you can be filled—you just have to seek.

God, I am sitting here before you asking you to fill me. I don't have the words for an eloquent prayer, or the equipping for great faith, but I do have the heart to be filled by you. Show yourself to me today.

Altar of Sacrifice

While God was testing him, Abraham still trusted in God and his promises, and so he offered up his son Isaac and was ready to slay him on the altar of sacrifice.

HEBREWS 11:17 TLB

Have you ever received a promise from God only to then be led to relinquish it? Isaac was Abraham's son of promise—a dream given by God, granted—now demanded in offering. Why would God give us vision and promise and then ask for us to lay that same dream down on the altar? Perhaps it's because it's only in the crucifixion that we find the resurrection. In the laying down and the dying that we find the abundant life of salvation.

Lord, give me the strength to follow you in obedience no matter what you ask of me. I know that in sacrifice you bring praise and that in ashes you bring beauty. Help me to trust you with the dreams that are closest to my heart.

Strength

It is God who arms me with strength and keeps my way secure.
He makes my feet like the feet of a deer he causes me to stand on the heights.
He trains my hands for battle; my arms can bend a bow of bronze.

PSALM 18:32-34 NIV

God may require us to do something that we don't feel equipped for, but he will always give us what we need to accomplish it. We may wonder if he chose the wrong person, or if we didn't hear his call correctly, but God can enable us to take on any task necessary to further his kingdom.

God, help me to trust you to accomplish your will through me even when I don't feel adequate. Help me to stop focusing on my own faults and instead fix my eyes on your strength.

Worthy

"You are worthy, O Lord,
To receive glory and honor and power;
For You created all things,
And by Your will they exist and were created."
REVELATION 4:11 NKJV

Worship is our natural response to the goodness of God. It's not simply an emotional reaction—worship is also the act of offering back to God the glory that he rightly deserves. When we stop to think about God's power, majesty, and creativity, we cannot help but glorify him because he is so worthy of the highest form of honor.

By glorifying God in our daily lives, those around us will take notice and some will ultimately be led to join us in praising him.

God help me to praise you in the way that you are worthy of. Help me to respond to you with honor, appreciation, and worship. I want to look for you in everything, so I can give praise back to you for all you've done.

Return

"If you return to the Lord, your brothers and your sons will find compassion before those who led them captive and will return to this land. For the Lord your God is gracious and compassionate, and will not turn His face away from you if you return to Him."

2 CHRONICLES 30:9 NASB

When we have sin in our life, it can be tempting to run from God and hide. We don't want him to see our weakness, and we fear his judgment. Our sin creates a barrier in our hearts between ourselves and God. It blinds us to his mercy and grace.

Covered in shame, we are without the confidence of a child living in freedom. But the Lord beckons us to return to him, promising compassion, grace, and restored favor.

God, no sin is more valuable to me than my relationship with you.
Give me the strength to overcome, and to once again live in right relationship with you.

Who Do You Say I Am?

He continued by questioning them, "But who do you say that I am?"
Peter answered and said to Him, "You are the Christ."

MARK 8:29 NASB

We must determine who we say Jesus is. Even Peter, who had walked closely with Jesus, was still asked this potent question: "Who do you say I am?" We can follow Jesus, walk with him, even be a devout follower, but who do we truly believe he is in our hearts?

Our belief about who Jesus is has a direct impact on our relationship with him. Do we believe he is our salvation and our only hope? Jesus' identity cannot change no matter who you believe him to be: he is the Messiah, the son of God—undeniably. But who you say and believe Jesus is will make all the difference in your heart.

Lord Jesus, I believe that you are the son of God—my savior.
Help me to live a life that loudly speaks to that belief.

Your Eyes Will See

Your eyes will see the King in His beauty;
They will behold a far-distant land.

ISAIAH 33:17 NASB

On the difficult days when our faith is weak, our tears flow freely, and our hearts are discouraged, we wish just to see God. We think that if we could look into his eyes, have the chance to ask him our deepest questions—and hear them answered—then we could continue on.

Beloved, the reality of heaven is closer than we can imagine. We will see our King, in all his greatness and his beauty. We will look upon that distant land of heaven. We will one day dwell there in peace: with every question answered and every tear dried.

Thank you God, that you have promised heaven to me through my belief in your son. Thank you that I will see your face one day and walk with you in your kingdom. When the days are hard, help me to remember that in just a little while all will be well and I will be with you.

Ruled by Emotion

Then we will no longer be immature like children. We won't be tossed and blown about by every wind of new teaching. We will not be influenced when people try to trick us with lies so clever they sound like the truth.

EPHESIANS 4:14 NLT

God has called us to be overcomers. He desires for us to stand firm in what we know to be true, rather than to be ruled by our varying emotions. As we mature in Christ, the truth of God's Word will come to carry more weight in our hearts than our own feelings do.

Lord, thank you for giving me emotions. My emotions draw me to you in love, help me to call out for you in sadness, and lead me to praise you in joy. But I thank you that because of your truth I am no longer at the mercy of my feelings. I can rightly discern the truth with a clear mind.

Unhindered

Because of Christ and our faith in him,
we can now come boldly and confidently into God's presence.
EPHESIANS 3:12 NLT

Our salvation awards us the great privilege of being able to approach God unhindered. With sin no longer dividing us from his holy presence, we are free to bare our souls to God as his beloved sons and daughters.

As bold and confident lovers of God, there is nothing we cannot share with him—and he with us. Fear and shame have no place in this kind of excellent love.

I love you, Lord. I praise you that you made a way for me to love you unhindered. I don't want my fear and my shame to interrupt our relationship, so I ask you to take it from me. Show me what it means to be a bold and confident child of yours.

Focus

I have set the Lord continually before me;
Because He is at my right hand, I will not be shaken.
PSALM 16:8 NASB

The mark of a purposeful life is strong focus. When we fix our eyes on a goal, we are far less likely to become distracted by conflicting interests. By setting the Lord continually before us, we become fixated on the greatest possible purpose.

This resolution of focus steadies us; we cannot be shaken, deterred, or destroyed while we are so firmly positioned toward Christ. There are few things more powerful than Christians who have determined to allow nothing to hinder them from achieving God's purposes and plans.

Lord, I want you to become my singular goal. Remove the little gods from my life that threaten to distract me from my highest purpose. Thank you that I cannot be shaken with you as the Lord of my life.

Fulfilling God's Dreams

Only let each person lead the life that the Lord has assigned to him,
and to which God has called him. This is my rule in all the churches.
1 CORINTHIANS 7:17 ESV

God created you perfectly to be the person he planned for you to be. He has plans for your life and purposes for your talents. When we long to be someone else, or somewhere else, we miss out on the incredible plan that God has for who we are right where we are.

By devoting ourselves to live the life we've been called to, we fulfill God's excellent dream for our lives. There is no greater privilege than to honor our creator by living out the purpose he planned for us.

Lord, I want to bring you honor in the way that I live and glory in how I use my unique talents. Make your calling clear to me so that I can fulfill it.

Found in a Desert

He found them in a desert,
a windy, empty land.
He surrounded them and brought them up,
guarding them as those he loved very much.

DEUTERONOMY 32:10 NCV

Do you ever go through seasons in your life where you just feel dark? Perhaps directionless or uninspired? In a metaphorical wilderness where you can't get a glimpse of any vision or even hope, God can find you. Even in the deserts of your own heart where you can't muster the strength to reach out to him, he can and will meet you.

Wait for the Lord, even in your emptiness; wait for him and he will come for you.

Thank you, Father, that you are near to me even when my heart is broken and my strength has failed. Thank you that you find me in my wilderness and you will restore me to joy.

God of Compassion

The Lord is good to everyone.
He showers compassion on all his creation.
PSALM 145:9 NLT

The good things in your life—material, internal, spiritual, or social—are expressions of God's regard for you. When God looks upon you, his heart fills with compassion… and he is always looking upon you.

God comforts and heals you when you are broken and hurting. He doesn't have a hot temper, he never breaks any of his promises, and he always does the right thing. Moreover, if you honestly call on him, he runs to your side.

God promises he will grant your desires, hear your cries, rescue you, and protect you—all because you love and fear him. Take heart; Jesus loves you!

Death to Life

God, being rich in mercy, because of His great love with which He loved us, even when we were dead in our transgressions, made us alive together with Christ.
EPHESIANS 2:4 NASB

Every autumn, summer's deep green leaves fade into a thousand shades of gold and red. Their fiery beauty lasts for a few weeks but eventually browns and falls to the ground under the weight of the wind. Trees shake barren in the cold, already anticipating spring and the buds which will once again decorate empty branches.

A simple, yet seemingly harsh, law of generation: there must be death for there to be new life. Mirrored by creation, we all have things in our lives which need to die in order for new life to be breathed on us. Old habits, negative relationships, damaging thoughts—whatever must die so that the new life in Christ can grow is well worth the exchange.

Father, though the process of dying to the old things is painful, I know that the new things to come are worth far more than what I'll leave behind.

The End of Death

He will swallow up death forever. The Sovereign Lord will wipe away the tears from all faces;
he will remove his people's disgrace from all the earth.
ISAIAH 25:8 NIV

How beautiful it is to think that all we fear and all we've been ashamed of will someday be erased. Death, our ultimate enemy, will be swallowed up completely when God has his eternal victory.

When we have put our hope in the Lord, we have the most incredible promise ahead of us. Any temptation to despair or to become overwhelmed with our present circumstances should disappear when we remember the hope we have ahead. We are partakers in a hope that knows no sorrow, children of a King who knows no defeat.

Thank you, Lord Jesus, that you will swallow up death forever.
Thank you that one day you will wipe every tear from my eyes,
and I will know firsthand the overwhelming joy and victory that is mine in you.

Comfort for the Failure's Heart

Now may our Lord Jesus Christ himself and God our Father,
who loved us and through grace gave us eternal comfort and good hope,
comfort your hearts and strengthen them in every good work and word.

2 THESSALONIANS 2:16-17 NRSV

God doesn't leave us alone in our weakness. When we feel incapable, he gives us the strength we lack to accomplish the task. When we are working sincerely for him, our work—no matter how insignificant it may seem—will always be effective.

We may feel like a failure in the eyes of those around us, but in the eyes of the Lord, our work done for his kingdom is never wasted. He cares enough about our hearts to comfort us in times of failure, and to value us in our moments of insignificance.

Lord, sometimes I feel that I have disappointed you. Despite my weakness, you comfort my heart and strengthen my soul. I know that in your eyes, I am never a failure. I am forever your beloved child.

Father Knows Best

This is the confidence we have in approaching God: that if we ask anything according to his will, he hears us. And if we know that he hears us— whatever we ask—we know that we have what we asked of him.

1 JOHN 5:14-15 NIV

Our prayers are not offered up to a silent heaven. When we pray, we are heard by a God who cares deeply about what we bring before him. By understanding the depth of his interest we gain confidence to approach him boldly in prayer.

God is a good Father who will not be swayed into giving us anything that is not to our benefit. We can present our requests to God freely knowing that if what we ask for is not what is best for our lives, then it will not be given to us.

Thank you, God, that you answer my prayers in accordance with your perfect will. Help me to trust that you know exactly what is best for me.

The Giant Obstacle

David said to the Philistine, "You come to me with sword and spear and javelin; but I come to you in the name of the Lord of hosts, the God of the armies of Israel, whom you have defied."

1 SAMUEL 17:45 NRSV

When young David met the champion Goliath in battle, he was so focused on the Lord that the giant who stood before him became nothing more than an obstacle to be overcome. Even when the voice of the giant taunted David, he was unaffected because his trust was securely placed in the almighty God.

We must let God overcome the giants of self-doubt that try to keep us bound in complacency.

Lord, help me to be so focused on you that the voices of negativity that enter my mind would pale in comparison to the overwhelming confidence that I have in you.

Kindness Leads to Repentance

"Love your enemies, and do good, and lend, expecting nothing in return; and your reward will be great, and you will be sons of the Most High; for He Himself is kind to ungrateful and evil men."

LUKE 6:35 NASB

If kindness is what leads to repentance, then we must first be kind to the unrepentant. Throughout Scripture we see examples of the kindness and mercy of God toward those who don't deserve it. All of us, at one time, were ungrateful and evil—but God still pursued us with his excellent love regardless of our position. It was his unrelenting kindness that brought us to our knees.

We who have been forgiven of so much must testify of the grace we've been shown by extending it freely to those who still find themselves in darkness.

Thank you, Lord, for the kindness you've shown me that ultimately brought me into your kingdom. Help me to love others as you love me.

Filling the Emptiness

O God, you are my God; earnestly I seek you;
my soul thirsts for you; my flesh faints for you,
as in a dry and weary land where there is no water.
PSALM 63:1 ESV

We all experience seasons where we feel emptiness: an ache deep within us that is inexplicable but present all at once. In those times, when we aren't sure what it is that we're longing for, it is more of God that we need.

Deep in the heart of every person, there is an innate need for intimacy with our creator. Without it our souls literally faint for want of him. But the beautiful truth is that he longs to fill us with himself. We have only to seek him in expectation.

Lord I long for your presence. I need you desperately. I pray that you would meet me in my emptiness and fill me with your Spirit.

Same Spirit

The Spirit of God, who raised Jesus from the dead, lives in you. And just as God raised Christ Jesus from the dead, he will give life to your mortal bodies by this same Spirit living within you.

ROMANS 8:11 NLT

The Spirit of revelation that reveals mysteries of eternity is the same Spirit that speaks to you. The Spirit of power that makes blind men see is the same Spirit that heals you. The Spirit that makes dead men live is the same Spirit that brings you to life.

As a believer, the Holy Spirit of God literally dwells within you and transforms every facet of your life.

Thank you, God, for putting your Spirit within me and enabling me to live a life worthy of your calling. Thank you that you didn't leave me dead in my sin, but awoke me to everlasting life. Help me to live with a present knowledge of the power I possess through your Holy Spirit.

You Make Him Happy

The Lord will not forsake his people, for his great name's sake,
because it has pleased the Lord to make you a people for himself.
1 SAMUEL 12:22 ESV

What could be more rewarding than to know that you please the Lord? When you enter into a relationship with God, he promises to never leave you. He's with you for the long haul, not only because it's not in his nature to leave, but also because—simply put—you make him happy.

Often we convince ourselves that we have disappointed God. This translates into shame in our relationship with him. But God is pleased with us, and he longs to speak that over us. Spend time today delighting yourself in the Lord, and feeling his delight over you in return.

What a beautiful thing to know that I bring you pleasure, God.
Thank you for making me one of your people and for promising to never leave me.

November

When the storms of life are raging,
Tempests wild on sea and land,
I will seek a place of refuge,
In the shadow of God's hand.

He will hide me, He will hide me,
Where no harm can e'er betide me;
He will hide me, safely hide me,
In the shadow of His hand.

Tho' He may send some affliction,
'Twill but make me long for home;
For in love, and not in anger,
All His chastenings will come.

Enemies may strive to injure,
Satan all his arts employ;
He will turn what seems to harm me
Into everlasting joy.

He Will Hide Me
By M. E. Servoss

Wise Home Construction

"Everyone then who hears these words of mine and does them will be like a wise man who built his house on the rock. And the rain fell, and the floods came, and the winds blew and beat on that house, but it did not fall, because it had been founded on the rock."
MATTHEW 7:24-25 ESV

Every wise builder, regardless of what region of the world they come from, know the most important piece of building a home is the location of the foundation. That is why Jesus admonishes us to build on rock and not sand. In good weather, both locations might look sturdy. One might not see the inherent weakness of hard, dried sand.

But the earth doesn't stay hard and dry. Rains, floods, and winds come at their own whim, and this is when location matters the most. What looked strong at first quickly comes crashing down when the floor turns to sinking sand. In this parable, Jesus makes it clear that *both* homes will see violent storms. The house built on the rock is not immune to hardship. But where it will show itself strong is in the fact that it cannot be destroyed because it was built on the right foundation.

Father, help me not to be dismayed in storms—for they strike us all. Help me be encouraged that I won't fall because I chose to build my house on the right foundation.

Not As the World Gives

I leave you peace; my peace I give you. I do not give it to you as the world does.
So don't let your hearts be troubled or afraid.
JOHN 14:27 NCV

For children, gifts tend to be the highlight of parties. As a child, you like having friends celebrate you, and eating cake drenched in copious amounts of frosting is fun, but the act of opening presents is the real joy of a birthday party. Perhaps this is sadly lost on adults. We "mature out" of wanting gifts, thinking we are too old. Scripturally though, God seems to be the eager parent, anxiously waiting for his children to draw near to him so he can impart gifts. He loves to give.

Jesus is the only one able to give true peace, and he loves to give it to us. Receive today gifts from the Father that only he can give. He might not be giving you what you think you want, but he is giving you gifts that will sustain and satisfy your heart.

Father, thank you that you don't give as the world gives; you are better than that.
Help me receive your peace as a gift from a great dad to his child today.

Stronger for Waiting

They who wait for the Lord shall renew their strength.
ISAIAH 40:31 ESV

Have you ever waited on someone? When you wait, you abdicate your ability to determine when something will happen. You are dependent on someone else.

When we wait on God, it can be incredibly difficult. Truly waiting on him means we aren't solving situations on our own. We wholly place our dependence and trust in God's solution, knowing it will be better than ours or anyone else's. Waiting is not natural. We would much prefer to act, even at the risk of acting incorrectly, than to wait on God. Even if we've waited a week or twenty years, his promise to us remains: if we persevere in waiting, we will become stronger.

Father, give me the fortitude to remain steadfast in my waiting. Thank you for your promise that I will be stronger if I wait.

Collected Tears

You have seen me tossing and turning through the night. You have collected all my tears and preserved them in your bottle! You have recorded every one in your book.

PSALM 56:8 TLB

Our grief is near to God's heart. He longs to console us: to stroke our hair, wipe our tears, and whisper comfort. He counts the nights we toss and turn; he collects our tears. God isn't absent in our sorrow, rather the opposite—he is closer than ever.

Don't be afraid to come to God with your grief. Share with him the deepest feelings in your heart without holding back. In his presence you will find comfort, hope, compassion, and more love than you could imagine.

Thank you, Jesus, for holding me in my sadness. I need your strength even more in my grief. Please be near to me and comfort me in your presence.

Outwardly Wasting?

So we do not give up. Our physical body is becoming older and weaker,
but our spirit inside us is made new every day.
2 Corinthians 4:16

Aging isn't a valued trait in much of the Western world. Entire industries gross millions of dollars each year to help disguise age. Tell-tale signs of aging like hair color and skin elasticity are not seen as a badge of honor but something to hide. We don't even like to acknowledge our age because it is virtuous to look younger than we actually are. Is this a Biblical or worldly concept? Have you indulged in the lie that you have been fed?

Ancient cultures, like the Hebrews, have a more Biblical view of aging. Aging is honored because it means you have endured and persevered longer than others. Often with age comes wisdom, and that is to be admired. One thing we cannot do is stop the aging process. But with age comes inward renewal and beauty for followers of God.

Thank you, Father, that as I age, I am inwardly being renewed. I won't remain in this body forever. One day, I will receive a new resurrected body that will never grow old. I'm excited for that day!

Light and Momentary?

Our light and momentary troubles are achieving for us an eternal glory that far outweighs them all.
2 CORINTHIANS 4:17 NIV

Let's be honest, how many of us would be offended to have a dear friend tell us our troubles were light and momentary? Perhaps some troubles really are light and momentary; they only last for a few moments, and by night you hardly remember them. Maybe you ran out of gas on your way to the store, or you were late to a meeting. But have you buried someone you loved? Have you been abandoned by those you trusted? Can those troubles still be considered "light and momentary"?

Biblically speaking, they can. This is because *all* trouble in this life is considered light *when compared to* our eternal glory. If we can grasp that this age is temporary and will pass before we know it, then we will better be able to weather the troubles that happen here. When we step into the eternal, glorious age to come, we will confidently say that the glory we see there far outweighed every trouble experienced here.

Father, help me set my hope in your promise of the age to come. I ask for your grace to believe that whatever trouble I am experiencing, it is indeed light and momentary.

My Gift

*Like good stewards of the manifold grace of God,
serve one another with whatever gift each of you has received.*
1 PETER 4:10 NRSV

We most commonly think of a gift as something that is given to us for our own enjoyment and benefit. But in the kingdom of God, a gift is given to a person for the enjoyment and benefit of others. What could be more Christ-honoring than to give our gifts away so that others can be blessed?

If the church is to grow and be edified, then selfishness can have no place in it. Each time we use our own gifts to better others, we are retelling the gospel with our lives.

Lord, give me the courage and wisdom needed to use my gifts to further your kingdom. I don't want to waste the gifts you've given me. Show me how my specific gift can be most useful to you.

Hope of Glory

God decided to let his people know this rich and glorious secret which he has for all people.
This secret is Christ himself, who is in you. He is our only hope for glory.

COLOSSIANS 1:27 NCV

Let's take a moment to contemplate true strength. Your body may feel weak to you on a day-to-day basis. But, if you are a child of God, you are not the only one indwelling your body. Christ is in you, and *that* is the hope of glory.

To walk in the knowledge and peace that Christ is in you, by his spirit, is abiding in a place of enormous strength. We know that Jesus is greater than anything and anyone. Acknowledge the powerful truth that if you are born again, Christ is dwelling in you. The same power that raised Jesus from the dead also rests in you—and that will be the power that raises you with him on the day he calls you to your eternal home. Indeed, this is the hope of glory.

Father, thank you for giving me your son's Spirit and making me alive in you.
Let me not forget that radical truth.

328

Rewards or Wrath?

> "Store up for yourselves treasures in heaven, where neither moth nor rust destroys, and where thieves do not break in or steal."
> MATTHEW 6:20 NASB

In this life, you can, and do, make a direct impact on your life in the age to come. The Bible teaches a lot on the principle of storing up various things for the eternal age. When you store them, you don't see them now. You set things aside, either consciously or unconsciously, to receive in eternity. It is your retirement package for the age to come.

Stubborn people with unrepentant hearts actually store up wrath. This shouldn't scare believers because they have approached God already in humility and repentance. For believers there is much better news: they are storing up rewards. Let's store up treasures that won't rust—to be enjoyed for all eternity.

Father, give me the faith to store up treasures now while I can.

No Longer Infants

This work must continue until we are all joined together in the same faith and in the same knowledge of the Son of God. We must become like a mature person, growing until we become like Christ and have his perfection.

EPHESIANS 4:13 NCV

When we first come to Christ, we are babies in the faith—regardless of our actual age. As God begins his work of making us like him, he feeds us gentle baby food. While infants are adorable, they aren't meant to stay that way. God matures us by his Spirit, feeding us food that we have to chew. This food is meaty and it satisfying but we have to process it.

The passage in Ephesians 4 refers to our maturing through solid teaching of the Word of God. Many teachings of Jesus are simple to hear but hard to do. A mature child of God can receive and do what God asks without being offended. Infants aren't mature or grounded in the Word. They are susceptible to being tossed back and forth by poor teaching. Praise God that it is his work to mature us!

Father, help me not resist your discipline and training in my life.
I don't want to be tossed back and forth by false teaching. I want to be mature in you.

Mind Control

If people's thinking is controlled by the sinful self, there is death.
But if their thinking is controlled by the Spirit, there is life and peace.
ROMANS 8:6 NCV

Our minds are a powerful tool. No action takes place, whether good or bad, without starting first as a thought in the mind. Your mind dictates your entire body. What you give your thoughts to has direct implications on the actions you take. God calls us to be transformed by first renewing our minds so we will rightly discern his will.

But controlling and renewing our minds isn't natural to us. Often we feel helpless or subject to the thoughts that come through our brains, and we find ourselves entertaining them without even being conscious we are doing so. That is why God has given us the most necessary and precious gift—his Spirit. Apart from his Spirit, we are powerless to steward our thoughts well. When his Spirit controls our thoughts, we'll find that our minds move from anxiety, fear, and death to life and peace.

Jesus, please fill me with your Spirit. I submit my mind to you today and ask you to control it so that my thoughts become those of life and peace.

Separated from His Love

Know therefore that the Lord your God is God; he is the faithful God, keeping his covenant of love to a thousand generations of those who love him and keep his commandments.

DEUTERONOMY 7:9 NIV

Has someone ceased to love you? What was the offense that put their love over the edge? Too many infractions? Too much broken trust? Your apology did not seem sincere? Maybe you have ceased to love someone. Human love is frail. This is why it is all the more critical not to put human attributes on God. His love is nothing like ours.

Enjoy your Father's steadfast love today. His love is incapable of failing you because nothing has the power to separate you from it. Don't berate yourself for your fickle love; be strengthened in his unfailing love.

Thank you, Lord, that your love is incapable of failing and I cannot be separated from it.

Gift of Weakness

When Uzziah became powerful, his pride led to his ruin. He was unfaithful to the Lord his God.
2 CHRONICLES 26:16 NCV

King Uzziah became King of Judah when he was 16 years old. 2 Chronicles 26 speaks highly of him as he began his young reign as king. He did what was right in the eyes of the Lord and as long as he sought the Lord, God gave him success. But something changed part way through his reign. His strength actually became his weakness. It led to pride and his ultimate destruction.

Have you ever considered that your weaknesses might be gifts from God? They might be what forces you into humility because you know that you aren't perfect and are always in need of a savior. God resists the proud, but the humble in heart can draw near to him. Which are you?

Father, thank you that you give grace to the humble. Thank you for my weaknesses that allow me to cling even more closely to your precious cross. Help me to embrace humility and draw nearer to you.

Talking Back

Who indeed are you, a human being, to argue with God?
Will what is molded say to the one who molds it, "Why have you made me like this?"
ROMANS 9:20 NRSV

Have you ever found yourself talking back to God? We do so when we think we know better, or when we think we see more clearly. We sometimes think our earthly wisdom exceeds that of our maker. We might talk back when we are sincerely hurting over tough—and sometimes tragic—circumstances.

It's not that God isn't thick-skinned enough to handle our questions. They don't rattle him or make him insecure. But often they don't help us an ounce. Spiritual maturity shows when you can whole-heartedly acknowledge to God that you don't understand but you still trust him. He is love. Everything he does is love. You can count on that.

Father, thank you that you are good. Help me trust you when I think I know better.

Were You There?

> "Where were you when I laid the foundation of the earth?
> Tell me, if you have understanding."
>
> JOB 38:4 NRSV

Have you been in a spiritual storm? Storms are painful because they expose our weakness and doubt before us and God—and sometimes others. Often God uses, and sometimes even creates, storms so that he can have our undivided attention.

God isn't being cruel to Job in his questioning. He is helping Job see that God is much bigger. If God was capable of orchestrating the intricate design of the earth, then surely he is capable of leading Job's life with the same care and wisdom. Even though it might look otherwise, God is to be trusted. Listen for his voice in your storm.

God, thank you that you are so much bigger than I am. Help me to understand that since you were capable of creating the world and all its intricacies, you are equally capable of caring for me.

Discipline as a Gift

No discipline seems pleasant at the time, but painful. Later on, however,
it produces a harvest of righteousness and peace for those who have been trained by it.
HEBREWS 12:11 NIV

We all appreciate well-disciplined children. Children that have learned, at some point, that they must submit to their parents are a delight to be around. While they are still fully children, they exhibit a humility that submits to rules and authority—even when they don't like it.

As children of God, we can also take comfort when he disciplines us. The heart of God in disciplining us is clearly that he does it in love, for our benefit. He is serious about dealing with sin in our hearts, and this will naturally be painful. But we should be encouraged; if we submit to the discipline of God in our lives, he gives us a precious gift—a harvest of righteousness and peace. Who doesn't want a more peaceful heart?

Lord, help me embrace your discipline.
Train me by it so that a harvest of righteousness is produced in my heart.

Running Unhindered

Since we are surrounded by such a great cloud of witnesses,
let us throw off everything that hinders and the sin that so easily entangles.
And let us run with perseverance the race marked out for us.

HEBREWS 12:1 NIV

Have you ever watched a runner hindered by added baggage? In the Olympics, do you see runners racing with a backpack on their back? Hiking boots, jeans, coats, or sweatshirts? No. Trained runners run as leanly as they can. They wear aerodynamic shoes, sleeveless shirts, and thinly weighted shorts. Their goal is to not be hindered by anything so they might run the best possible race.

The author of Hebrews correlates our Christian pilgrimage to that of a runner in a race. We have the power to make our run much easier. The Holy Spirit is excellent at specifically showing us what is hindering us. We weren't designed to run a sluggish race—sin and disobedience cause that. Through the Spirit's power, you can throw off *anything* that hinders you and run.

Father, give me the grace and strength to cast off sin, so I can run my race in the best possible form.

God Loves Justice

Now let the fear of the Lord be upon you. Judge carefully,
for with the Lord our God there is no injustice or partiality or bribery.
2 CHRONICLES 19:7 NIV

God had set up a system for Israel and Judah to manage themselves as a nation. Part of that system included setting apart judges who would rightly and wisely rule when there was a dispute. His call to the appointed judges was powerful. For a nation that was created to represent and be a blessing to the world, it was really important for them to have just judges. They represented God.

Do you long for justice in a specific area of your life? How about for the countless disenfranchised victims in the world? You must know that your passion for justice comes from God's heart. Not everything looks fair and equitable right now. But this isn't the end. Your just Judge will judge the world rightly when all is said and done. Even more mind-blowing is that he already judged us by pouring his wrath on Jesus on the cross, so none would have to pay the ultimate price for our sin.

Thank you, God, that you love justice. Thank you, Jesus, that you suffered on my behalf so I don't have to suffer the full weight of my sin. Your love is truly perfect and I am deeply grateful.

Stored Goodness

How abundant are the good things
that you have stored up for those who fear you,
that you bestow in the sight of all,
on those who take refuge in you.
PSALM 31:19 NIV

David, who enjoyed a great friendship with God, makes many wonderfully startling claims about God. God is storing up goodness! What exactly is that goodness? Is it safety and security? Is it peace in trials? Is it a quiet heart in the middle of a storm? Is it joy in the midst of mourning? Yes, it would seem that his goodness could be all of these and much more.

There is so much goodness that God actually has to store it, so he doesn't drench us in it all at once. But there is a caveat. The goodness referenced in this passage is reserved for a special group of people—those who fear God. It is for those who humbly come to him because he is the King and they are not. Rest assured, God will reward you more than your wildest dreams for loving him like that.

Help me, Jesus, to trust in God's goodness like you did when you were on the earth. Thank you that you see my faith even when it's weak, and you store up goodness for me.

*L*earn from Me

> "Come to me, all you who are weary and burdened, and I will give you rest."
> MATTHEW 11:28 NIV

Perhaps it's morning when you are reading this. Your day is just beginning, yet your heart is already heavy. Or maybe it's the end of the day and you feel weakened by the burdens you have taken on. Rest in the kindest person there ever was. Let his words soothe and strengthen you.

Perhaps you have taken on more than what God is asking you to—physically or emotionally. Christ himself makes it clear that his yoke is easy and his burden is light. If your yoke is too heavy, perhaps you aren't supposed to be carrying it in the first place. Learn from Jesus. Refusing wrong yokes won't necessarily feel natural to you. But ask and learn. As you do, he will strengthen your ability to know the difference, so you might enjoy his rest.

Jesus, help me learn from you and rest in you. I don't want to carry any yokes that you aren't asking me to. Give me wisdom and discernment as I walk into each new day.

A Friend in Him

"I no longer call you servants, because a servant does not know his master's business. Instead, I have called you friends, for everything that I learned from my Father I have made known to you."

JOHN 15:15 NIV

Pharisees knew the Law but rarely knew the spirit of the Law. There are many issues where they were passionate about obeying the Law, but their hearts were far from God. This is a dangerous place to be. God is far more interested in a humble and a contrite heart than cold-hearted obedience to his Law with a bitter spirit.

Have you ever found yourself obeying the commands of God but with a heart that was far from his? Be careful of this tendency. We can sometimes be rule-keepers without walking in deep friendship with God. God is not just looking for a servant; he is looking for a friend. Servants obey because they have to. Friends walk in close relationship because they understand shared love.

Holy Spirit, only you can reveal Jesus to me and help me see him in his humility and love. I pray that you would help me to obey the Father not out of duty but out of love.

Ask, Seek, Knock

"Ask and it will be given to you; seek and you will find; knock and the door will be opened to you. For everyone who asks receives; the one who seeks finds; and to the one who knocks, the door will be opened."

MATTHEW 7:7-8 NIV

Has your faith gotten weaker over time? Have some of your harder experiences left your more faithless than hopeful? Remember, regardless of the degree of your hard experiences, he promises to work everything out for good in your heart and life. Don't let your disappointments cloud the truth of God's Word. He promises that everyone who asks in his name receives.

Are you asking? Then you can count on receiving. Are you seeking? He promises you will find. Are you knocking? Yes, child, the door will be opened to you.

Father, please refresh me by the truth of your Word.
Help me to believe you again and with faith ask, seek, and knock.

Calling and Selection

Be all the more diligent to make certain about His calling and choosing you; for as long as you practice these things, you will never stumble; for in this way the entrance into the eternal kingdom of our Lord and Savior Jesus Christ will be abundantly supplied to you.

2 PETER 1:10-11 NASB

Peter had just shared a crucial piece of wisdom for believers: when you have faith, be good. When you are good, be knowledgeable. When you are knowledgeable, be self-disciplined. When you are self-disciplined, become tenacious. When you are tenacious, become godly. When you are godly, become warm-hearted toward each other. When you are warm-hearted, become a lover. What a list!

Why did Peter continue to warn us that we should ensure we are called and chosen? Because to require a journey from faith to love is impossible, but to live and dwell in Christ makes for a fully satisfying, joy-filled journey. When you stumble, Jesus helps you up. When you are weak, he is strong. Assess your heart, and trust Jesus to it. Choose his blood for your power, grace, and mercy, and his presence as your constant companion. Stay in the journey fully dependent upon Jesus and all he is.

Jesus, I choose you!

*G*rowing in Discernment

See to it that no one takes you captive through philosophy and empty deception, according to the tradition of men, according to the elementary principles of the world, rather than according to Christ.

COLOSSIANS 2:8 NASB

The simplicity of the gospel can be offensive. This is because it relies solely on Jesus' complete work on the cross and not on our own merit. We are saved purely by receiving Christ's payment for our sins. He was able to pay for them fully because he provided a perfect sacrifice for the sins of all of mankind.

There are many false teachings that will try to lead you away from simple faith and trust in God's ability to save you. The responsibility to discern and not be taken captive by false teachings is on us. We have be rooted and grounded in the teachings of Jesus so that we can discern the difference between false teaching and the teachings of God. Let us build our faith wholly on Christ.

Father, help me be rooted in your teachings so I can better discern the counterfeit.

Committed to the Process

Put on your new nature, and be renewed as you learn to know your Creator and become like him.
COLOSSIANS 3:10 NLT

While our salvation is a completed work, there is a continual working out of our faith. This is because God has called you into a relationship with himself. Relationships need to be nurtured and maintained. The word the Bible uses for this concept is *renewal*.

Even after salvation, our new self is still being renewed in knowledge in our creator's image. Our minds also need continual renewal. Don't be discouraged if you are still struggling with old ways of thinking or acting. Renewal is a process. Continue to repent and submit yourself to God. He is more passionate about renewing you than you are. He's a loving God who is committed to the process.

God, I'm sorry for all the times I fall short. Help me to continually seek to renew my heart and my mind. Show me how to become more like you.

Content in All Situations

I have learned how to be content with whatever I have.
PHILIPPIANS 4:11 NLT

What an incredible gift Paul walked in. He knew how to be content regardless of how much or how little he had. It's interesting too that, as a believer, both situations arose in his life. There were times he had plenty and times he didn't. Did that mean God wasn't blessing him when he lacked? No, it simply meant those were the circumstances he found himself in. But you hear no accusatory overtone in Paul's writing here. He is not angry at God. He simply understood that following God would, or could, mean times of plenty and times of scarcity.

The secret to contentment is realizing that our circumstances don't determine our peace. We might be suffering or we might be on a mountaintop of victory, but our peace and our steadfast walk with God remain the same either way. Our joy is not contingent on our circumstance. Rather, we are satisfied that God will give us what we need when we need it.

God, I trust that you know exactly what I need. You are a faithful provider and I thank you for the many blessings you have bestowed on me. I choose to be grateful for the times of plenty and the times of want. Help me to be equally content in both situations.

Standing Blameless

To Him who is able to keep you from stumbling, and to make you stand
in the presence of His glory blameless with great joy.

JUDE 1:24 NASB

Have you ever noticed what people did in Scripture when they were in the presence of an angel? Often they fell down, or they were so taken aback by the angel's presence that they had to be told not to fear. If that is what people do when they see angels, how do you suppose we will react upon seeing God himself? God calls us to stand before him. How will we even breathe?

Beloved, that we can stand blameless with great joy is an amazing truth that should cause us to arise with tears of gratitude. God does this for us because he no longer counts our sins against us. He has judged his Son in our place and has given us his Son's righteousness. We are blameless in his presence not because we don't sin, but because Jesus has paid for our sins.

Thank you, God, that you alone will cause me to stand in your presence perfectly blameless.
Thank you for receiving me and calling me your own.

A Confident Approach

Let us then approach God's throne of grace with confidence,
so that we may receive mercy and find grace to help us in our time of need.
HEBREWS 4:16 NIV

Children were given parents so their basic needs could be met. It is a parent's job to provide food, shelter, and clothing. In a healthy home, if the children need anything else, they know they can go to their parents any time and make a request for what they need. This is especially true in crisis. If there is an urgent need, or a difficult situation, nothing delights a parent more than to see the child run to them to get help and wisdom.

That is a small picture of what God wants us to do with him. Are you in need? God invites you to *confidently* approach his throne. You need not be timid when you approach him; he says he will give you the mercy and grace you desperately need. Don't be afraid. You can confidently approach God in your hour of need.

Thank you, God, for your invitation to approach your throne with confidence.
Help me understand how much you love me and desire to meet my needs.
Thank you for your endless supply of grace.

Origin of Strength

"People do not live by bread alone, but by every word that comes from the mouth of God."
MATTHEW 4:4 NLT

When Jesus was tempted by the devil, he had been in the wilderness fasting for forty days and forty nights. He wasn't consuming any calories during that time. Instead, he was giving all his energy to communing with the Father and being strengthened by their relationship. At the end of that time, Satan came to tempt him. Jesus withstood authentic temptation and never gave in.

It's interesting how God prepared Jesus for this trial. He didn't have him attend a conference, read a self-help book, or have a healing service. Instead, he led his son to be physically weaker so he could lean fully on the Father. Jesus had been on a 40-day diet of love, affirmation, and encouragement. He wasn't weakened by his lack of food. In fact, he made it clear that food alone wasn't what made a child of God strong. Perhaps that's one of the greatest gifts in fasting—we are able to see that it isn't food that sustains us but God's power in us.

Father, thank you that we don't live on bread alone. Help us eat what we need to be strong in you: every Word that comes from your mouth.

The First Move

We love because he first loved us.
1 JOHN 4:19 NIV

Before Jesus began his earthly ministry, he was baptized by John the Baptist. John's job had been to prepare the way. Before Jesus was even on the public scene, he was calling people to repent. He would then baptize them. Jesus went to John to be baptized like many others, but he did this before he did anything else that was noteworthy. Yep, no miracles, no healings, and no deliverances are recorded from him prior to his baptism.

Immediately after he came up out of the water from his baptism, God spoke for all to hear: "This is my Son, whom I love; with him I am well pleased" (Matthew 3:17 NIV). What had Jesus done thus far? Nothing. He was simply God's son. Yet God's words to him were that of affirmation and love. Perhaps that's how God relates to us—his other children. He loves us because we are his. And we love him because he loved us. It's just that simple.

Father, help me respond and be restored by your simple love.
You have made the first move in loving me. Please strengthen me by your love.

December

For Thy mercy and Thy grace,
Constant through another year,
Hear our song of thankfulness,
Father and Redeemer, hear!

Dark the future; let Thy light
Guide us, bright and morning star:
Fierce our foes and hard the fight;
Arm us, Savior, for the war.

In our weakness and distress,
Rock of strength, be Thou our stay;
In the pathless wilderness,
Be our true and living way.

Keep us faithful keep us pure,
Keep us evermore Thine own;
Help, O help us to endure;
Fit us for the promised crown.

For Thy Mercy and Thy Grace
BY HENRY DOWNTON

Peace in Jesus: the Eternal Gift

*"Give glory to God in heaven,
and on earth let there be peace among the people who please God."*
LUKE 2:14 NCV

Christmas trees might be secular decorations, but they invoke, in Christians, thoughts of a more precious tree: the cross. Jesus came to us on Christmas day for the purpose of bringing peace to his people through the cross of Calvary.

Christ's mission was to redeem us from every thought, word, or action that didn't match up to our God-likeness. He destroyed our sins and silenced our enemy, permanently, on the cross. He empowered us for victory. Each of us carries his glory as a child of the Most High God. This is a Christmas gift for each of us to open every day.

Holy Father, thank you for this gift. Please toss out the broken ornaments of my life, and remake me according to your glory. Give me peace. I affirm you as my Lord. Thank you for loving me so tenderly. I love you, too.

DECEMBER 2

Execute Your Hope in Faith

"When you see the ark of the covenant of the Lord your God with the Levitical priests carrying it, then you shall set out from your place and go after it.... Do not come near it, that you may know the way by which you shall go, for you have not passed this way before."
JOSHUA 3:3-4 NASB

Joshua stood at the cusp of the Promised Land. The Lord had spoken; the Israelites would consecrate themselves and then follow the Ark of the Presence into their promise. They would take God's new route to get there, so the vast camp traveled far behind the Ark, allowing each citizen to see it and faithfully follow God for themselves. In this manner, each Israelite successfully executed the actions of their faith before God rather than man. Led in the presence of God, every man crossed the Jordan, felled Jericho, and enjoyed the life of milk and honey promised him.

Today, each of us faces decisions that position us toward the fulfillment of God's promises in our lives. We take courage, consecrate ourselves, and follow him. Jesus has given us our land. We step into it, running the race with Jesus, and securing our hope. This day is our present opportunity.

God, I want to follow your Word and be led forth in peace.
I prayerfully engage you in this journey and ask you to help me keep my eyes always on you.

353

The Love-Joy Life

"As the Father has loved me, so have I loved you. Abide in my love. If you keep my commandments, you will abide in my love, just as I have kept my Father's commandments and abide in his love. These things I have spoken to you, that my joy may be in you, and that your joy may be full."
JOHN 15:9-11 ESV

Joy comes into our lives through actions of obedience. Moreover, we may obey God for the sake of righteousness, but God rewards us for it by baptizing us in his love! As we abide in this love, we become vessels of joy, spilling onto dry places in the world around us. That joy will consume us, becoming a hallmark of his righteousness.

Strength and courage rise in the context of God's joy. We pursue and choose his ways, gaining fortitude to overcome, and we begin to live the supernatural life. In following the faithful one who overcame the world, we become like him, and we overcome as well.

Thank you, Lord, for hearing my cry for mercy. You are my strength and shield. Thank you for loving me. Help me to abide in your love.

Water of Life

"Whoever drinks of the water that I shall give him will never thirst. But the water that I shall give him will become in him a fountain of water springing up into everlasting life."
JOHN 4:14 NKJV

Sometimes, we need "extra." Our spiritual requirements are never met by earthly experiences. When these experiences occlude our spiritual opportunities, we leave off from them, thirsting. Life as expected derails—whether from internal failures or external events—and this creates great inner struggle. The verve inside us may dwindle in the face of such difficult challenges. Where will we get joy and strength to continue?

Jesus says he brings us abundant life *wherever* the enemy has tried to kill, steal, or destroy. He is just that faithful. His living water is an endless fountain. We reach up to him, relying upon him to fill us with this eternal life.

Jesus, I praise you. Thank you for being good to me and loving me. Please pour your "extra" into my thirsty soul as I pour your holy Word into my life. Envelop me in your presence, and train me to stand in you as a relentless and immoveable child of your joy.

Lay Down False Expectations

This is how we know what love is: Jesus Christ laid down his life for us.
And we ought to lay down our lives for our brothers and sisters.
1 JOHN 3:16 NIV

Part of laying down one's life rests in relinquishing inappropriate expectations. When the highlight reel of your mind doesn't match your life, you hand that reel to Jesus. He returns to you belonging and peace. These two blessings hinge upon your identity in him, not upon your attempts to achieve.

God places his desires within the hearts of his holy ones. When they are ignited, these desires produce good things: creativity, productivity, and charity toward others. You are not a failure. You are a possibility—*God's possibility*—opening up in the light of Jesus like a flower in sunshine, coming into its full bloom.

Thank you, God, that my life is not a mistake but a unique expression of your nature. Help me to be myself and live according to who I am, not according to expectations that create an ill-fitting yoke.

Charity

If anyone has material possessions and sees a brother or sister in need but has no pity on them, how can the love of God be in that person? Dear children, let us not love with words or speech but with actions and in truth.
1 JOHN 3:17-18 NIV

Christmas season is filled with opportunities to give. More so than during any other time of the year, charities offer venues for community service and vehicles for giving to others. In response, we drop money into buckets, tuck gifts under angel trees, and say extra prayers for those in need. In addition, we may find ourselves watering flowers for traveling neighbors or hosting a dinner party for those without family. Being a soft spot for those bruised souls in our path is a mark of discipleship.

Nobody wants to be alone or hungry on Christmas. Nobody wants to give their kids regretful hugs instead of gifts, shelter, or homemade food. In a time of hope and gladness, your active love reaches beyond the circumstances of the afflicted.

God, may my hands and my supply bless the hearts of those who are in need this season. I ask you to give of yourself through me. Help me to be a willing vessel of your blessing to those who so desperately need it.

$\mathcal{F}$reed: for Life

"Let any one of you who is without sin be the first to throw a stone at her."
JOHN 8:7 NIV

If you feel Jesus is holding back his love and compassion from you because of something you have done or not done, think again! When Jesus died on the cross, he mercifully forgave you.

Forgiveness is only appropriate when someone has done something wrong, so God isn't hung up on your sin. Instead, God hung your sin on a cross and set you unequivocally free! Enjoy living.

Jesus, you didn't condemn the woman caught in adultery,
and you don't condemn me even though I deserve it. Thank you.
Help me to leave my sin behind and be fully cleansed by your work on the cross.

Known of My Father

So they were saying to Him, "Where is Your Father?" Jesus answered, "You know neither Me nor My Father; if you knew Me, you would know My Father also."

JOHN 8:19 NASB

The Pharisees were taunting Jesus. They knew Joseph was only his step-father, and they threw his earthly status in his face. Why? Because he unraveled them. He unraveled them with his compassion, his love, and his willingness to associate with people they wouldn't touch. He didn't do things their way, and he called them out for being unholy. He didn't make sense to them, and he certainly didn't change to make them comfortable.

You're really not that different from Jesus. You are a stranger to this world, and because you inhabit it, all heaven breaks loose, and the earth gets set on its head. You might not see this for yourself, but it's true. That annoys some people as much as it blesses the rest. Take courage! Jesus understands you, sees you, and chooses to draw you even closer as you seek him.

Papa, thank you for making yourself my real dad. I could never have imagined a better one. Knowing this gives me strength and a grateful heart to remain true to your purposes. Thank you for Jesus, who showed me what to do. I love you so much.

Steps to Intimacy

Shout for joy to the Lord, all the earth.
Worship the Lord with gladness;
come before him with joyful songs.
Know that the Lord is God.
It is he who made us, and we are his;
we are his people, the sheep of his pasture.

PSALM 100:1-3 NIV

King David celebrates God. He worships him, gladly, singing songs to him. This sets David's heart in proper perspective. He knows who God is and what he has done for his people. David knows his identity through the Lord, his creator. He recognizes God's value and thereby his own.

When we encounter God's worthiness, we should experience gratitude, and echo that back to God. We can be overcome with God's goodness, his love, and his everlasting faithfulness.

God, I shout for joy to you. You have made me yours and I cannot contain my thankfulness. I worship you for your goodness and love. Thank you for all that you have blessed me with.

God Provides

Then God said, "Behold, I have given you every plant yielding seed that is on the surface of all the earth, and every tree which has fruit yielding seed; it shall be food for you."

GENESIS 1:29 NASB

God gave us the first recursive gift: plants which bear seeds. He then told us to multiply and farm the land. In doing these two things, God provided for our food needs and took on the heavy lifting in turning seeds into food. He didn't do it for any reason beyond his love for each one of us.

We plant, we water, we weed, yet God creates the miracle. We can take delight in playing a very small part in our providence. Why? Because God loves to collaborate with us—and oftentimes what he wants to do is greater than we can ever imagine.

Thank you, God, for planting seeds in my life. Thank you for watering them and helping them develop into good fruit. Thank you for meeting my needs and letting me play a part in your process. I trust you with my life.

Emotions

There is an appointed time for everything. And there is a time for every event under heaven.
A time to weep and a time to laugh; A time to mourn and a time to dance...
A time to embrace and a time to shun embracing... A time to be silent and a time to speak.
A time to love and a time to hate; A time for war and a time for peace.

ECCLESIASTES 3:1, 4-8 NASB

God's emotions are on full display throughout Scripture. He has made us in his image. He understands our form, our emotions, and our frailties.

In his kindness, he gives Biblical instruction regarding how and why we handle emotion appropriately. He teaches us to express or conceal it, and to administer our responses in righteousness. What a loving God we have: that he would lead us into emotional strength and freedom.

Jesus, your emotions toward me are caring, tender, and very good. As I abide in you, I know your Holy Spirit will lead me into all knowledge regarding how to wisely administer my emotions. I submit myself as your steward in this vital area of life. Thank you for your kind guidance.

Making Choices: a Good Gift

Out of the ground the Lord God caused to grow every tree that is pleasing to the sight and good for food; the tree of life also in the midst of the garden, and the tree of the knowledge of good and evil.

GENESIS 2:9 NASB

God created the tree of life. He made all things, and he made all things good. He declared them good. So how was the tree of the knowledge of good and evil good? God gives us choices. Just like you can't make anyone love you, God won't try to make you love him or obey him.

These are choices you make for yourself, and he designed this from the beginning.

Jesus wants us to bring him into every part of our beings, thus choosing life. As new creations, we have nothing left but to trust him, to judge what is good, and to do it.

Thank you, God, for giving me the choice to love you. I choose you again today.
You are perfect in all your ways, and your plan is good.

He Teaches Me Acceptance

"I have brought you glory on earth by finishing the work you gave me to do."
JOHN 17:4 NIV

As we walk in love as faithful children, we will see fruit develop from what we do. We bring life and joy, truth and gentleness. We bring our gifts and ambitions. Often, this is met with delight and gratitude. Other times, people don't understand our intentions. Still other times, we sow our gifts faithfully, and never see good come of it. The gifts God gives us are a portion of a legacy that cannot be recognized in a generation. You may be feeding the poor, heartbroken there is not enough water. You may be clothing the naked, weeping that their bills won't be paid this month.

The point is this: you are being faithful. God is proud of you. And though the world around you may not understand what you are doing, and though you may not understand the world around you, Jesus has everything handled. He is making beautiful things in and with you. That is enough. Just walk with him in faith.

God, there is so much of the world I don't understand. Some of it I don't want to know. Make me bold to trust you and to know that everything will be okay as I rest in you and walk in life.

He Is a Triune God

In the beginning was the Word, and the Word was with God, and the Word was God. He was in the beginning with God.

JOHN 1:1-2 NRSV

Have you ever opened up a bar of chocolate and broke off just one rectangle? That rectangle was surrounded by others that looked just like it. Each linked in with its mates to form a consolidated whole. Separately and collectively, the chocolate held the same essential properties throughout that gave it identity. One would consider this chocolate in terms of multiples or a whole, but the fact remained the same: it was all glorious chocolate!

God is a bit like a chocolate bar. Whether he breaks off a piece that comes to earth, or enters the person who believes, it is very much true that if we have experienced him in some form, we have experienced the gracious Father who is seated on the throne of heaven. Each person of the Godhead is not at all a cookie cutter of the others, but these three persons agree completely, separately, and as one. They are—he is—God!

God, when I experience you, I taste and see that you are really, very good. Thank you for breaking off a piece of your precious self, in the form of Jesus, on Christmas day. Today, I celebrate your triune sweetness in my life!

_____

_____

_____

_____

_____

_____

_____

He Blesses Me Eternally

How blessed is the man who fears the Lord,
Who greatly delights in His commandments.
PSALM 112:1 NASB

Blessings from God are gifts given as a result of his grace toward us. We can grow in God's graces just as we grow in the graces of the people around us. When we revere him and abide in his love, we naturally obey him from the heart. As our hearts knit together with God's, this grace improves.

The Lord keeps you steadfast, secure, and ultimately triumphant as you fear and obey him.

Lord, please train my heart to fear and honor you in everything I do.
I want to know your intimate and sovereign presence, to cling to you in it,
and to become a rich and timeless blessing to you and the people you touch through me.

Filling the Hole

> "Don't store up treasures here on earth where they can erode away or may be stolen. Store them in heaven where they will never lose their value and are safe from thieves. If your profits are in heaven, your heart will be there too."
> MATTHEW 6:19-21 TLB

If asked, you could probably come up with several causes for temptation. Sooner or later, most people might gravitate toward blaming the devil for at least a few of their woes. But what about looking at ourselves? Sometimes we fill the void with whatever is handy: material objects, prestige, experiences, or relationships.

Have you ever thought about how that void grows more like an abyss every time you toss a new item into it? It is sobering. If we do not seek God at that opportunity, we try to plug the hole with distractions until we are lost in an endless sea of distress. Each believer is given Jesus and his Word, so we can navigate back to the only one who truly fills our souls.

Lord, I praise you! Thank you for your Word which has the power to change me. Please transform me by it as I read and remember your message. Replace all those empty or ill-filled places in my life with what you say, rather than with earthly ambitions, activities, and artifacts.

He Chooses the Proper Time

"My dear Martha, you are worried and upset over all these details! There is only one thing worth being concerned about. Mary has discovered it, and it will not be taken away from her."

LUKE 10:41-42 NLT

Martha's problem was not that she was a hard worker but that she neglected the correct choice when it was laid before her. Hospitality is a great gift, and it will be useful to change your world. But right now, if God wants to speak with you personally, it is time to drop everything and listen. Sit at his feet, and let him provide for you as you have need.

Moses had a busy job as a shepherd. Yet, he stopped everything, one day, when he saw a burning bush. He could have just praised God as he walked along. Instead, he entered into a phenomenal partnership with God that changed the world.

Father, thank you for calling me to yourself. Please train my heart to be sensitive toward you. I want to rest at your feet, hear your voice, and feel your breath on me as you speak. I love you, I bless you, and I thank you.

He Delights in You

The Lord directs the steps of the godly. He delights in every detail of their lives.
Though they stumble, they will never fall, for the Lord holds them by the hand.
PSALM 37:23-24 NLT

Jesus lives in you by choice. He has saved you quite capably. He is excited merely by being with you. Jesus doesn't need you to earn his gladness. He promises to calm your fears in his love. He is so happy that you exist that the very joy of it causes him to burst forth into singing as he dances and twirls about you.

You are encompassed and filled with God's no-holds-barredd delight... in you.

Thank you, Jesus, that you are the maker and redeemer of my soul.
Thank you for your unabashed joy toward me. I am in awe of your goodness.

Blessed Enemies

Feed your enemy if he is hungry. If he is thirsty give him something to drink and you will be "heaping coals of fire on his head." In other words, he will feel ashamed of himself for what he has done to you.

ROMANS 12:20 TLB

Amongst nomadic and rural populations, fire remains essential to survival. If someone's fire goes out, they must scurry to the stoop of a neighbor. Clay pot balanced on her head, she hopes for life-giving fire. If the neighbor loves her, she will heap hot coals into that jar, and the household will be saved.

God says his goodness brings people to repentance. They feel shame at the disparity between their motives and people who give them mercy. For this reason—for mercy and reconciliation—we heap up unlikely kindness on the very ones who hurt us. We leave that kindness as a jewel in Jesus' hand: a token that softens hearts where needed. As the flames of mercy spring up for a cold heart, we steal death from the enemy, and create opportunities for reconciliation and peace.

God, show me where to do this. I want to make something good of the bad situations I've faced. I hand them over to you. Soften my heart so I serve those you would gently and kindly bless through me.

His Understanding Illuminates Motives

A plan in the heart of a man is like deep water,
But a man of understanding draws it out.
PROVERBS 20:5 NASB

Sometimes we fail to understand people's motives. They get in our faces, grate on our nerves, and disrupt our peace. In fact, we can, at times, question their authenticity. The Bible says you will need understanding to figure people out.

Wisdom means knowing what to do, and understanding means knowing why.

According to the Word, you ask, read the Bible, and pay attention to what happens around you in order to make strides in both. Be pure-hearted and receptive as you pursue, and you will learn a great deal. You will discover what questions to ask yourself and others to get to the root of a motive.

Jesus, thank you for knowing all things and for sharing your mind with me. Make me wise and understanding, please. As you teach me, change my heart to be like yours.

He Offers Gifts Unreservedly

David asked, "Is there anyone still left of the house of Saul
to whom I can show kindness for Jonathan's sake?"
2 SAMUEL 9:1 NIV

In the story of David, we meet an infirmed grandchild of Saul named Mephibosheth. Because of Saul's cruelty to David, Mephibosheth would have been an unlikely candidate for David's favor. David had the heart of God, though. For the sake of his friend, Jonathan, David granted Mephibosheth a regular seat at his table as well as his grandfather's entire estate and the servants he needed. David extended luxurious favor upon one who could not possibly benefit him, and who did not think himself a friend.

It is true: God is quizzically kind and compassionate to all people, regardless of how they stand with him. Although you may feel you have let God down, or you have little to offer, Jesus invites you to his feast table every day. He welcomes you to stay in his presence so you will enjoy the lavish care he continually gives you.

Lord, thank you for loving me so well. Please show me your grace and mercy, and help me to extend it, as I bubble over in your goodness. Make me wise in all things, Father.

He Dresses You for the Weather

Put on the new self, created to be like God in true righteousness and holiness.
EPHESIANS 4:24 NIV

You have such a beautiful future ahead of you! What a blessing it is that you will affect people by just being you: lovely, holy, and loved of God. Because you are a child of God, your home isn't here. It's in heaven, where spiritual weather is always fine. If you go out into an earthly storm, you change your inward clothes to meet the earthly challenges before you.

Earth isn't your home turf; life here is laden with storms. Fortunately, Christ has given you ample covering for the weather. Put on the new man to overcome with Christ. He has offered it to you, and he finds it precious that you wear the clothing he provides.

Jesus, thank you for empowering me to put on the new self and discard the old. Thank you for overcoming the world and offering for me to dwell safely in your light's protective warmth. I will walk in faith as the storms of life blow around me.

He Chooses You as You Are

God chose what is foolish in the world to shame the wise; God chose what is weak in the world to shame the strong; God chose what is low and despised in the world, even things that are not, to bring to nothing things that are, so that no human being might boast in the presence of God.

1 CORINTHIANS 1:27-29 ESV

When Christ gathered his dream team for spreading the good news across the globe, he prayerfully selected young and inexperienced men who had nothing to recommend them. He sidestepped experienced people to fill the role with someone who would need to trust him and listen closely in order to succeed. Matthew was a customs official, but Jesus charged Judas with taking care of finances. In Acts, Jesus called Gentile Peter to convert and serve the Jews, while Pharisee Paul was sent to the Gentiles.

Even today, God has this principle: he is so pleased with you walking in his trust that he uses you to make his name great in unlikely places—often where you cannot go in your own strength. Trust him to tell you where and to guide you as you go.

Jesus, I know you call me. I trust you and want you to train me to hear your promptings. I will listen, and ask you for strength and understanding as I obey.

Seek, then Boldly Proclaim!

They hurried off and found Mary and Joseph, and the baby, who was lying in the manger. When they had seen him, they spread the word concerning what had been told them about this child, and all who heard it were amazed at what the shepherds said to them.

LUKE 2:16-18 NIV

When the shepherds were told about Jesus, they didn't pencil him into their schedules; they ran to him! They ran as fast as their feet could carry them. Who watched over the sheep? Who knows! But in that moment, they knew the importance of the Lord's advent, and they rushed to Bethlehem, and into his barn stall, to see him. Once they saw him, and experienced him, they rushed to tell of him. God didn't choose earthly leaders to spread the word. He chose messengers who would faithfully carry the good news.

Who is this Lord of ours, that fishermen and ranch hands spread his good news? Hallelujah! Christ has come! Tell your friends! Tell your neighbors! Tell everyone you meet: Jesus is the Lord, and he has come in the flesh! Hallelujah!

Lord, thank you for coming to exchange beauty for ashes, joy for mourning, and praise for heaviness. I sing to the world with all my soul, "Glory to God in the highest heaven!"

Jesus: My Christmas Song

"The Root of Jesse will spring up, one who will arise to rule over the nations;
in him the Gentiles will hope." May the God of hope fill you with all joy and peace
as you trust in him, so that you may overflow with hope by the power of the Holy Spirit.
ROMANS 15:12-13 NIV

Jesus, a Jew, came so all people would be qualified to experience his indescribable hope, joy, and peace as they placed their faith in him. It's not a wonder that a great band of angels joined together in praise that night. Jesus is the true basis for every believer's hope and joy, for this season and for all time.

You may be alone today or with many people. You may be reading this Christmas day, or you may be catching up after a flurry of activity. Perhaps you are flipping through this book, and you've stopped on this passage. Wherever you are, and whatever your circumstance, you have a gift from the Lord for this very day. It's okay; a Christmas gift from God doesn't expire! The gift God has for you, each and every day, is this: he is your strength and your song. And he always will be.

Jesus, thank you for being my Christmas song. You are in touch with what I need to fill my soul even when I do not know. Thank you for your kindness in coming to earth so I could become your child. The thought of this fills my soul with gratitude and praise.

_____

_____

_____

_____

_____

_____

_____

God's "No Returns" Policy

God never changes his mind about the people he calls and the things he gives them.
ROMANS 11:29 NCV

The days and weeks after Christmas can be an awkward mess. In one instance or another, we find we've given or have been given a gift that is unsuitable or wrongly sized We may have overlooked someone entirely. The recipient may stand in line at a store for a return or write a letter of thanks for something that, at best, caused a moment of humor.

Isn't it refreshing that God, in his great understanding and thoughtfulness, gives gifts appropriate to us: gifts that do not cause regret? Moreover, these often produce gifts we give to the world, and back to God.

What has God entrusted to you that you've thought too big to handle? What will you do, today, to begin that journey? God refuses to regret his selection of you for the task.

Jesus Frees Me from Anger

People with understanding control their anger;
a hot temper shows great foolishness.
PROVERBS 14:29 NLT

We've all snapped. We must be wise in our anger, though, because it may destroy the protections God has built into our lives. Anger is a response to suppressed fear, humiliation, rejection, or pain. Getting to the root of these events allows us to deal with anger, disarm, and move forward, unencumbered. Jesus isn't cruel: he doesn't want you to be mishandled. He will reward you as you submit to him, responsively, in times of both peace and injustice.

Wrath is vengeful anger which retaliates rather than reconciles. We thwart the devil by casting wrath, anger, vengefulness, and bitterness from our hearts and choosing kindness, tenderheartedness, and forgiveness.

God, I know there are areas where anger has gripped me. Please show me the real emotions behind my flare ups, and illuminate my heart to your perspective toward each event that has caused me pain. I choose to see circumstances through your eyes and to think as you do.

He Is My Steadfast Hope

We know that in all things God works for the good of those who love him,
who have been called according to his purpose.
ROMANS 8:28 NIV

Not everything starts out being God's idea for your life, but he makes beautiful things of it, in spite of that. The good God has in mind might not even be on your radar yet. But if the love of God is peaceable and kind, then surely his gifts are in step with that.

Sometimes, it is hard to imagine life being good after our world gets swayed. True to form, God is faithful in the midst of it, and he has plans that defy your expectations. Take comfort, and choose to hope for the future and for your good.

Dad, I know you are right here. I see you in the wind blowing through the trees, and I trust you to hold me through every circumstance, even as you keep the earth spinning in motion. Troubles try to unravel my hope, but I know better than to let them! You work everything out for good, and I trust you.

Source of Beauty

Do not adorn yourselves outwardly by braiding your hair, and by wearing gold ornaments or fine clothing; rather, let your adornment be the inner self with the lasting beauty of a gentle and quiet spirit, which is very precious in God's sight.

1 PETER 3:3-4 NRSV

"Pretty is as pretty does," women often tell their girls. Why? Because curling our hair, buying trifles, and improving clothing, posture, and speech isn't where beauty is found. Jesus coaches us in beauty. Peers and magazine articles address our appearances, distracting from the valuable person within.

Beauty shines from within. It dresses in humility and true wisdom. It grows in an environment of reverent, holy living, thriving in worship and glorifying God. It is embodied in Christ and his heart toward people. It is good to look nice, and sometimes our gifts or calling require it. But we need to keep holiness our central focus as we offer our appearance to God. We are meant to be adorned with his beauty.

I want to be beautiful, Lord. Knowing my heart waxes beautiful as I revere you properly, I follow you in quiet peace, asking you to inspect me, and gently reassign any ugliness hiding in my frame. Please help me become an ornament of your grace.

The Law of the Spirit

But the Holy Spirit also witnesses to us; for after He had said before,
"This is the covenant that I will make with them after those days, says the Lord:
I will put My laws into their hearts, and in their minds I will write them."
HEBREWS 10:15-16 NKJV

In the original Passover, the Festival of Shelters, the nation of Israel celebrated receiving the law. It was day fifty since they stepped foot out of Egypt, and they had seen mighty things at God's hand. As God handed Moses the law, he also told him that one day it would be written on people's hearts. Year after year, the Israelites celebrated this day by bringing in the first fruits of their fields: grain.

The year Christ was crucified at Passover, the disciples and followers of Jesus were gathered in the upper room. The promised Holy Spirit came and filled them, thus writing the law of the Spirit in their hearts. True to form, the first fruits of the harvest were brought in that day when three thousand souls converted at Peter's admonition to repent and be baptized.

Thank you, Holy Spirit, for your indwelling. Thank you for the peace and joy of your presence. Thank you for fulfilling your promise to write your laws on my heart. Help me to meditate on those laws and delight myself in them.

Load of Anxiety

Always be full of joy in the Lord; I say it again, rejoice! Let everyone see that you are unselfish and considerate in all you do. Remember that the Lord is coming soon. Don't worry about anything; instead, pray about everything; tell God your needs, and don't forget to thank him for his answers.
PHILIPPIANS 4:4-6 TLB

Carrying anxiety is like over-packing a car for a trip. Gas mileage suffers, companions have a hard time joining you, and blocked vision endangers your car and others on the road. Clearly, you need to unpack anxiety in order to free yourself for a better journey. So, what is the key to shaking anxiety from your life? Rejoice in God, and gratefully request his help with your encumbrances.

Fortunately, joy in the Lord is available in all circumstances. It's that jug of lemonade in your fridge which readily fills your cup. Rejoicing produces refreshment. Your problems become manageable because Jesus is invited into all areas of your life. He is your accompanying reality—anxiety can no longer take that seat.

I rejoice in you, Lord! All of my being praises you! You are good; you are kind. You constantly walk with me. I praise you, and I know you are sovereign over my circumstances. They will pass, but you will always be with me. Come and still my heart.